"That's _Still_ Not All, Folks!!"

"That's _Still_ Not All, Folks!!"

An autobiography by
Joe Alaskey

That's Still Not All Folks!!
© 2009 Joe Alaskey. All Rights Reserved.

All illustrations are copyright of their respective owners, and are also reproduced here in the spirit of publicity. Whilst we have made every effort to acknowledge specific credits whenever possible, we apologize for any omissions, and will undertake every effort to make any appropriate changes in future editions of this book if necessary.

No part of this book may be reproduced in any form or by any means, electronic, mechanical, digital, photocopying or recording, except for the inclusion in a review, without permission in writing from the publisher.

Published in the USA by:
BearManor Media
P O Box 71426
Albany, Georgia 31708
www.bearmanormedia.com

ISBN 1-59393-112-3

Printed in the United States of America.

Book & cover design by Darlene & Dan Swanson of Van-garde Imagery, Inc.

Contents:

	Foreword	ix
Chapter 1	How I Started Out As Other People (talent / kid stuff / first impressions / early influences & other impressionists / TV favorites)	1
Chapter 2	In Praise of Ham (growing up / what is ham? / more influences)	11
Chapter 3	Showdown with the Doomer (a high school horror story with a happy ending)	15
Chapter 4	Other Celebrities I Have Known and Loved (how to pronounce Albany / Paul Winchell / Joe E. Ross / Stan Lee & Steve Ditko / Norman Fell / Bob and Ray)	19
Chapter 5	I Get into Theatre — and Vice Versa (my mentor / college shows / first professional work / cars / why I dropped out)	29
Chapter 6	The Big Apple and The Worm (starving actor / NYC work / Hans Conried / Morgan Freeman / George Abbott / Tennessee Williams / Kaufman & Belushi / why I left NYC)	35
Chapter 7	The Boston Tee-Hee Party (early stand-up work / comedy colleagues: Steven Wright, etc. / Jay Leno / The Lenny Clarke Show / Martin Olson / more celebs / some of my bits / Jackie Gleason / silent comics / more bits / how I started a fashion trend / cartoon voices onstage / scouted by Friz Freleng)	41

vi   "That's Still Not All, Folks!!"

Chapter 8	So Then I Got a Day Job (radio work: the Loren & Wally Show / guests: Mickey Rooney / Henny Youngman / Soupy Sales / Carole King / Rich Little / Gordon Lightfoot / Larry Bird / Harold Russell / writing for Bob Hope / Lyle Talbot)	55
Chapter 9	On — and Almost Off — The Road (another horror story with a happy ending / Boston vs. NYC / talking to Gilda Radner / audition for Lorne Michaels / David Brenner's advice)	61
Chapter 10	Is Moose and Squirrel!! (meeting Bill Scott & June Foray)	69
Chapter 11	My Best Shot (going West / a broken heart / San Francisco Comedy Competition / A. Whitney Brown / the Improv & Budd Friedman)	73
Chapter 12	"Hi. I'm Francis." (celeb encounters: Howard Duff / Sahl, Dreesen & Robin / Bob Zmuda / Chuck McCann / Spade, Rosie etc. / David Frye / Jackie Vernon / G.L.O.W. / Dennis Miller & Ellen DeGeneres)	77
Chapter 13	Some Significant Signatures (first cartoon work: Return to Mocha with Bill Scott, June Foray, Daws Butler, Janet Waldo & Frank Welker / working with Bill & June: Spike Jones' band & Billy Barty / a correction / Bill's passing / first movie / Uncle George)	81
Chapter 14	Getting My Webbed Feet Wet (Bill Idelson & Richard Matheson / Jesse White / first Looney Tunes work: PSA / talent pool / Who Framed Roger Rabbit & Mel Blanc's legacy / WFRR: Mae Questel / Bob Hoskins / meeting Mel Blanc / Tiny Toons: audition / sciatica / name change / singing / co-stars / favorite episodes / guest stars: Carol Channing / Edie McClurg / Jonathan Winters / Steven Spielberg / Vincent Price / Don Messick / Mrs. Bush's Story Time / my spinoff)	85

Table of Contents　　*vii*

Chapter 15	Busy, Busy, Busy	101

(various v/os: commercials / Spitting Image / hired by Gleason / more Gleason work: Art Carney / proposed biopic / meeting William Shatner / Out of This World / D. C. Follies / guest stars: Larry Storch / Doug McClure & Golden Boot Awards / more TV work: sitcoms. stand-up & David Letterman / game shows: Win, Lose or Draw / Super Password / Hollywood Squares & Milton Berle / Match Game / Family Feud / Couch Potatoes: bits / Lois Lane & Jimmy Olsen / Jayne Meadows / Jay Leno

Chapter 16	You Can Do Anything in a Cartoon!! (Almost.)	119

(Mighty Mouse & Ralph Bakshi / Berke Breathed / more movies: Forrest Gump, Bob Zemeckis & Tom Hanks / Jack Lemmon / Blade / new agent / Sylvester & Tweety Mysteries / working with Chuck Jones: Father of the Bird / TimberWolf / Daffy Duck for President / musical work: Bugs Bunny on Broadway / Carnival of the Animals / awards / Space Jam / Tweety's High-Flying Adventure / Disney TV work / Baby Huey / Duckman / Rugrats: favorite episodes / Dad's reaction)

Chapter 17	Well, You've Got to Star Somewhere	135

(Lucky Stiff / celeb encounters near-encounters: Yarmy's Army & Don Adams / B. B. King / Joe Pesci / Sterling Holloway / Vincent Price / Ed Asner / Ed Wood / Gene Barry / Charlton Heston / Dennis Weaver / Orson Welles / Charlie Chaplin)

Chapter 18	Meanwhile, Outside the Looney Bin	147

(Ally McBeal, etc. / Nurses / more commercials / Casper / other TV: Nickelodeon / Carrotblanca / Cartoon Network: Time Squad / Harvey Birdman / Samurai Jack)

Chapter 19	The Day My Pants Fell Off in Public, or Names Aren't All I Drop	153

(LTs in gold / DD in 3D / Drew Carey / Looney Tunes Back in Action / Aflac / Duck Dodgers: behind the scenes / favorite episodes / the Emmy / more favorites / how my pants fell down)

Chapter 20	Who Said: "You Can't Go Home Again"? (one-man show / Bah! Humduck / that's a wrap)	169
Chapter 21	Dedication	177
List of Illustrations:	Oh, just thumb through the book, okay? It was hard enough just drawing them.	
Appendices:	(Woo!! Fancy word!!)	
	I. Joe Alaskey's Looney Tunes Checklist!!	181
	II. Joe Alaskey's Favorites	185
	III. Joe Alaskey's Tips On Doing Impressions	189
	III. A Joe Alaskey Short Story	193
	IV. Joe Alaskey's Got A Swelled Head	203
Blank, Usually		last page

Foreword

*W*ell, of course I wrote my own autobiography. I mean, what choice did I have? I tried writing my biography, but the dictionary wouldn't let me. Funny thing about me writing an autobiography, though — I don't drive a car!! (Thank you. Thank you very much.)

You can expect a lot more of these kinds of side-splitting jokes as you speed through this book, looking for your name. As a comedy writer who's written almost all of my own stand-up material, and much more besides, I've elected to kinda kid the whole process of jotting down one's memoirs, if you don't mind. (Too late now anyway.)

Hey, I don't know any better, all right? This is my first autobiography. But you only get one crack at Life. So to make up for that, I am now busy preparing my next 19 autobiographies.

To be serious for a moment . . . Okay, glad that's over.

Hey, I don't have to tell ya that the aforementioned Life we sorta share invariably holds both good and bad things that happen to everyone. And I've had plenty of both, thanks (though I admit I prefer the good things).

But if you think this book will be some kinda juicy, steamy, tell-all exposé or whatever, get real!! In a business like Hollywood and a town like Show Biz, everybody gets a pie. We all run up against bad luck, suffer bad timing, and make a few bad connections. This is news? If you wanna read *that* kinda depressing trash, pick up the tabloids at the check-out counter. Life is too short for all those negatives, and I'm a positive kinda guy . . . And I'm positive this book would be too long. Besides, the good things are more plentiful and interesting. The unfortunate missteps and circumstantial casualties of career competition get real boring to me. So I can imagine how you'd feel about it. Especially if you're reading this to glean any aspects of the splendid success that I've enjoyed thus far. Yep, this book is expressly for those who'd like to read about my twenty-plus years as the major voice of the Looney Tunes, and for those who'd like to learn how I developed as a voice actor and performer in general. As a human being, I prefer to keep my private life private, bub. Like most people.

But if you like Ham served with heaping side dishes of wild, name-dropping anecdotes marinated in curdled humor, then grab a paperback napkin and dig in!!

Joe Alaskey
December, 2006

Chapter 1:
How I Started Out as Other People

I never thought I'd become Bugs Bunny.

Or more correctly, I never thought I'd ever be able to deliver that voice, let alone feel the character of that amazingly funny and iconic cartoon character.

Daffy Duck? Yes. Getting him down was shamefully easy. All I did was —

But already I'm ahead of the story.

Let me go back to the beginning. (Hey, relax. Maybe some of you actually want me to.)

PORTRAIT OF THE ARTIST AS MR. POTATO HEAD

I knew I was an actor at an early age. You'll notice that the boldness of that statement includes no phrases such as "I knew I wanted to be" or "would be an actor someday." To heck with all that. As a matter of fact, even as a kid, I knew I'd never even need a lesson . . . !!

This all sounds terribly egotistical, doesn't it? Well, let me off that hook just long enough to say that to this day I've never felt egotistical about any talent or prowess I discovered in myself. The talent was just there.

So, so what? So it was up to me to do something about it, that's what.

I just started acting as soon as I could walk and talk. I was fond of dressing up as various characters, inspired chiefly by the polymorphous Mr. Potato Head, that tuberous master of disguise. I built and wore little pipe-cleaner glasses and construction paper mustaches, and even sniped cigar butts to enhance my portray middle-aged types, to my Mother Dorothy's undying bemusement.

"Why do you make all those faces and talk in all those funny voices?" she would ask.

And I would reply, "I'm actin', Mom!!" She warned me my face would stay that way. And she was right.

With childhood friends, I staged and promoted neighborhood shows (Westerns, war scenes, routines borrowed from the Three Stooges, Halloween monster-fests, etc.) and presented them in the family garage, complete with big cardboard boxes and Coming Attractions.

I remember showing "cartoons" by pushing multiple pictures I drew of my favorite characters up against a hole I cut for a "TV set" while doing their voices.

(As a natural extension of this activity, I later booked and screened cartoons and Laurel and Hardy shorts for fellow collegians in the late '60s.)

Also as a kid, I did impressions, practically from the moment I could speak, they tell me. I imitated anyone I saw on TV, and got spontaneous laughs from my versions of Jackie Gleason, Walter Brennan and Humphrey Bogart, just out of diapers. (Me, not them.)

I made Mom buy me comedy albums, which I memorized and would recreate at the drop of a hat (which people wore in those days). Imagine Steve Allen and his gang, Jonathan Winters, Victor Borge, Allan Sherman, Bob Newhart — all as a chubby five-year-old with glasses and a lisp. I "did" everyone I heard and thought funny.

But not Sylvester and Tweety. Not yet.

Although, being a blooming Baby Boomer, I was spellbound by animation. My earliest memories recall the original "Mickey Mouse Club," which aired classic Disney cartoons in black-and-white (My Mom sent away for one of the original mouse-eared membership hats), and a few local Saturday morning hours that played the Fleischers' Popeye, ancient Farmer Al Falfa and Scrappy cartoons (Look 'em up, young'uns!!), and, unsurprisingly, Warner Bros.' Looney Tunes and Merrie Melodies, voiced mostly by the mind-boggling Mel Blanc, which I still consider the funniest cartoons ever made for the movies.

With made-for-TV fare, I graduated from Huck and Yogi, having studied the differences between Daws Butler and Don Messick, to "Jonny Quest" in no time.

I suppose I tried "being" all my favorites as a toddler, and I must admit that the only one I can remember trying out and never getting even close to was Donald Duck. (To this day, I'm told my Goofy is right-on, however.)

Along the way, I lost the lisp and a tendency to stutter by reading out loud. This was a conscious effort on my part. As a result, I read a lot of books accidentally.

I only wanted to sound professional. After all, how else should a five-year-old actor sound?

As previously mentioned, I started writing and drawing cartoons around this time too. (Go ahead and thumb through the book. You'll find a few, as warned.)

And I watched a lot of movies, all kinds, all the time. I was insatiable, and still am.

Among these, my genre of choice was definitely the horror film, before graphic gore arrived and artistic sensibility strayed. Even then, their stars were iconic. I was riveted, and tried to re-embody their eerie escapades through continuous attempts to duplicate each one's creepy persona. I dearly loved them all, and still do. I still couldn't pick a favorite if I tried, from biggies like Bela Lugosi, Boris Karloff and Vincent Price (More about one of them later!!) to acquired tastes such as Dwight Frye, Lionel Atwill and George Zucco.

These amiable monsters relentlessly haunted my TV set and movie box offices as I grew up, and I supported them exhaustively, not only trying my best to get their voices and mannerisms down, but drawing them constantly and buying all the comic books and monster mags.

Forrest "Forry" Ackerman's *Famous Monsters of Filmland* magazine and I managed to scare my parents, at least. Later, it would be my literary excuses for *Playboy*.

On TV, the related genres of fantasy and science fiction were equally popular, so my renditions of Rod Serling and the many stars of "The Twilight Zone" — William Shatner, Burgess Meredith and John Carradine, for instance (More about one of them later too!!) — were also gleefully exploited by me, and not just for laughs. So I thought . . . !! (Hey, I was learning how to act, remember? I suppose I thought I'd like to be a horror movie star someday, but that was before horror itself became the only star of the genre.)

Meanwhile, my family loved me but wondered where all this fascination with Show Biz was coming from. Now and then, I myself wonder if reincarnation might explain me.

My older sister JoAnne and younger brother John Ned gave me

lotsa space as they pursued normal lives. Mom and my Dad Joe thought I was talented and gave me just enough space to explore my own interests, as long as I got good grades and kept the lawn mowed, all of which I did.

Everyone was impressed that little Joey the third wasn't a bit shy about performing (only about girls), started reading before he was three, earned an IQ score so high they wouldn't even tell my Mom, and got skipped ahead from kindergarten to second grade.

I wasn't so keen on that last item. Not that I didn't know why, or had trouble relating to kids just a little older, but I hated giving up my kindergarten desk onto which teacher had just put a nice new animal sticker. We all got a different one. And mine was a circus seal with a ball on the end of his nose. A performing seal. My Rosebud. I missed it terribly. (That and Irene Birmingham, age six.)

As a young reader, and while in grade school, I voraciously devoured not only the paperback mystery volumes touted by the then-ubiquitous Alfred Hitchcock, but many more, savoring novels and anthologies by such brilliant writers as Ray Bradbury and Richard Matheson, my personal favorite. (Annoyingly, here's my third more-about-one-of-them-later teaser!!)

So I started imitating other people at a very early age, before I'd ever seen a professional impressionist.

The first one I saw was the late Frank Gorshin, who was phenomenal. Will Jordan was the first to catch on in nightclubs with his hilarious and much-copied Ed Sullivan "really big sheww" bit (even copied by Sullivan himself!!), but Frank was the first to become a household name (in most of the houses I visited). He didn't "do" the deadpan variety show pioneer, but wowed everybody with his electrifying caricatures of Kirk Douglas, Burt Lancaster, Richard Widmark, Broderick Crawford, and scores more. And when I say 'caricatures', I mean it!! His comic style exaggerrated the physical and facial and vocal traits of

6 "That's <u>Still</u> Not All, Folks!!"

his subjects to a stunningly absurd degree, etched with a quivering intensity that barely contained his talent. For his depiction of Lancaster, he was all teeth and hands, speaking only in short, modulated bursts; and for his take on Sydney Greenstreet, to signify that famous paunch he somehow tilted his body backwards at 45° angle, literally bending over backwards to entertain us!! Sometimes the voices were a bit off, or the crowds were too stunned to laugh or applaud on cue, but Frank Gorshin was topnotch. When we met briefly just a few years before his passing, he was gratified to learn I knew his resumé practically by heart. He prefaced his autograph to me with: "Thanks for knowing so much about me!"

David Frye concentrated on scathing deconstructions of contemporary politicians, equally intensely as Frank, I should add. Like Jordan's Sullivan, his Richard Nixon and William F. Buckley, Jr. got under the national skin, and they're still doing his versions of them today.

Rich Little was everywhere: talk, variety and game shows, sitcoms, you name it. His friendly charm let him breeze through his repertoire, highlighting a few perfect portrayals like Jimmy Stewart and George Burns. He shortly outdistanced his colleagues in popularity.

It was no secret to insiders that Frank and David had drinking problems, a double damn shame. I met them both years later, both recovered. Mr. Frye had retired (though he returned on CD) and Mr. Gorshin returned to acting, which he'd always preferred anyway.

John Byner, who was the first to impersonate George Jessel and Johnny Mathis (among many others), was to me, although not as stylized as Gorshin, the funniest of the lot. A crossover into straight comedy as well, he did an original character he called Felix Fossadeedee (which he did in the animated feature *The Black Cauldron*), who has this high-pitched, querulous, throat-based voice which has been relentlessly recycled by other voice actors ever since. For the best-known example, nothing against actor Andy Serkis, but his Gollum in *The*

Lord of the Rings trilogy is an explicit vocal clone; to Byner fans, the similarity is inarguably obvious. (I like to think of it as homage.) For the record, in my heyday I worked with Byner when he hosted TV's showcase series "Comic Strip Live" in Hawaii, in which the producers and I offered a literal surprise tribute to the pint-sized polyvox. (Hey!! I just coined an important-sounding word!!) John's other gift is a casual, almost noncommittal feel to his work which kept me off-guard and watching for a smirk. (On my second CSL, I was the closing act.)

Coming along afterward were star specialists like the frivolous Fred Travalena (known best for his Jim Nabors) and genial George Kirby (who did Bill Cosby and Satchmo).

And many comedians who did more than impressions in their acts knew enough to do their best ones when they did, like the persistently funny Jack Carter, who did Ed Wynn and Maria Ouspenskaya (!!).

Classic comic actor and dialects-pert Larry Storch started the "Judy, Judy, Judy" Cary Grant line, worked for Jackie Gleason, played Mr. Whoopie (with Frank Morgan's voice) to his childhood friend Don Adams's "Tennessee Tuxedo" (which was his William Powell send-up, later used for Maxwell Smart), and encouraged and taught Sammy Davis, Jr. to do his impressions!! (Yes, more about Larry later.)

Last but not least, further mention must be made of the aforementioned Will Jordan, of whom I'd never seen enough. As physical as Gorshin, as intense as Frye, and as funny as any of them, he was the first to help define the hip, — and even "sick" — new comedy styles that sprang from the nightclub scene in the '50s. They all say that it all started with him, and after catching up to his work, I think it's yet another damn shame that this much-stolen-from genius never got more credit for his ground-breaking leadership in this field. (One can catch his astonishing Ed Sullivan in Bob Zemeckis's *I Wanna Hold Your Hand*.)

Throughout my career, I've met or spoken with all of these influential and very funny guys, and have found them all to be very bright and responsive, all very professional and all gentlemen. And if it weren't true, I wouldn't say it. (The only impressionist I ever met who wasn't one was a newcomer who stole most of my act -- and even then, he thought I'd enjoy seeing it!!)

Back on '60s TV, of which I definitely watched more than my share, this era's TV offerings were pretty wild, so doing comic impersonations from shows like ABC's "Batman" starring Adam West and Burt Ward followed as a natural progression of my mimetic predilection. This show in particular was abundant in vocal variety, richness and appeal; practically everyone on it was highly imitable. I can still go into Cesar Romero's Joker and Buzz Meredith's Penguin with no prep. And there was Frank Gorshin, of course, though his verbal gymnastics as the Emmy-nominated Riddler sustained a totally original characterization.

I was also an ardent fan of ABC's "Burke's Law" (1963-'65), which I've been telling people for decades was an unsung classic. It starred the versatile and sophisticated Gene Barry, who copped a Golden Globe for his multi-faceted work. The first show produced by Aaron Spelling, it was visionary in the fact that it was the first of the guest-star whodunit series (later revived by Messrs. Spelling and Barry for two more seasons in '94). Sometimes serious, often not-so, each week this unpredictable hour featured an average of half-a-dozen luminaries doing their best to look guilty. The show was very well done, with tight, witty scripts (a few by Richard Levinson & William Link, later the creators of "Columbo"), maintaining high quality throughout its run. I learned a lot about pure Show Biz and those who lived it while rapt in this show's clever machinations and flights of fancy. (DVDs, please!!)

Anyway, my garden of impressions was budding anew with their ever-changing "Special Guest Stars in Alphabetical Order," as I cultivated established names like Buster Keaton, Paul Lynde, Charlie Ruggles, Wally Cox, Louis Nye, plus up-and-comers Don Rickles, William

Shatner, Telly Savalas, etc. Then there were the babes!! Barbara Eden, Anne Francis, Elizabeth Montgomery, Mary Ann Mobley, Nancy Kovack, Janice Rule, Susan Oliver -- I watched every week!!

Ultimately, other terrific TV shows, late-night movies and my discovery of OTR (old-time radio) spurred a lifelong interest in nostalgia (at an unfortunate ebb of late). And all that homework has led to me to believe that the better half of the first century of recorded entertainments, despite all its flaws, belongs to the pioneers.

Chapter 2:
In Praise of Ham

So, having a penchant for performing and a flexible larynx, I was becoming an impressionist, whether I wanted to or not. (But I have to admit I did.)

My cousin Mark was the first to exploit my impertinent impersonations, requesting me to perform mostly at parties where everybody was already laughing anyway. Our favorite was by then an easy target, Ed Sullivan (based more on Byner's looser interpretation).

"Sullivanize me!!" Mark and our teenaged cronies would implore. And roar, as I hunched, frowned, swiveled, slurred, pointed needlessly, introducing people in the room as if they were sitting in his audience — without written material, mind you.

I indulged everyone and myself with other impressions, expanding my repertoire by just kinda picking up where the pros left off. I've been told I always had a knack for improvisation, though to this day, improv feels more like practice than performance to me.

But I thought I was becoming an actor.

At least a perceptible pattern was emerging as I grew particularly fond of, if not addicted to... ham.

Excuse me. I mean: Ham!! — In fact, make that *HAM!!*

This I admit with no apology, but in fact, with pride. And I'm not necessarily trying to be funny.

All good actors know how to be themselves. But it's entirely true that not every actor is capable of scaling Ham's lofty heights and maintaining one's artistic balance.

My favorites could do it, though, easily, gracefully, and most entertainingly.

And so I was determined to learn and promulgate this delicious theatrical tradition that is today woefully, unfairly regarded as "overacting." This is only the case when Ham is done artlessly.

Not that I think there's anything wrong with the Method either. Being one's self and mining that style works for many terrific actors, as we all know.

Yet I'd already seen quite overripe performances in the name of the Method, and figured out that overly self-conscious preparation and/or the complete dependence on one's own experiences to create a character, like scenery-chewing for its own sake, definitely limits an actor.

But as popular as the modern, ultra-realistic style has been in my lifetime, its universal adaptabilty to actors (from movie stars on up) has somehow curried favor with American culture to the point of an unfortunate dismissal of Ham as its equal in value.

How brrrutally unfairhh!!

The truth is that Ham is harder to do right.

Also, in the natural course of professional self-discovery, I felt and found that I had more to offer in losing myself in characters who are bigger than life.

And I knew that, as with Stanislavsky, Stella Adler, Lee Strasberg and Sandy Meisner, one must study and do one's homework to get Ham down just right.

Oh, I studied the Method method too, but quickly realized this was not to be my calling. Early in my high school years, I knew I would be a Ham, and only a Ham. Because of my belief in it, and my love of it.

In school and community theatre productions, as I began to adopt this very demanding but very rewarding technique as my own, other actors and performers of inspirational value blaringly called themselves to my attention. I was mesmerized by the gloriously oversensitive characters limned by Peter Lorre, Charles Laughton, Laird Cregar and Victor Buono.

Of course, an easy argument could be made that I gravitated towards emulating generous genii such as these because they all happened to be overweight, and so was I.

But it ran deeper than that. Orson Welles and Sydney Greenstreet didn't play oversensitive types. And neither had Vincent Price, Bela Lugosi, John Carradine, nor the great, sadly-underrated Hans Conried ever displayed double chins or problems with zippers.

Well, even with all this motivation, I knew I had to fashion an individual approach as an actor, so I strove not to copy my incidental instructors, but to develop "my own thing," as the saying went.

All through my teenage years, I was encouraged by friends to someday test myself in the world of stand-up comedy as a basic impressionist, which I sporadically did, for a few charity benefits and the occasional lark.

While I attended high school, reel-to-reel tapes were made by schoolmates of mine, and of these I was given — and still have — several lengthy demonstrations of my teenaged attempts at humorous apery.

There's one tape I wish I still had, though, especially because it made a big impact in my life and career-to-be.

Chapter 3:
Showdown with the Doomer

All through high school, I'm afraid I was infamous for my between-class-break impressions of not only everyone I could do from TV and the movies, but of the faculty as well.

A week before final exams, one of my parking-lot cronies talked me one weekend into immortalizing these routines on his big, clunky, grey reel-to-reel machine.

While the exams were going on during the last week before graduation, this wise guy waited for the Vice-Principal to leave his office, then snuck in and played that tape over the P.A. system. Not the whole tape. Just the impressions of the teachers.

I was not only astonished, I was mortified. Because I knew what was coming.

Within minutes, I was called into the Vice-Principal's office. This worthy gentleman's name was Brother Patrick. His nickname was "The Doomer", and he was well-known for expressing his displeasure with any given student in sometimes violent ways. He would slowly remove his pink-rimmed glasses, the signal for imminent mayhem.

And a particularly ridiculous and unflattering imitation of The Doomer was the headliner on this baby.

When I entered the office, the glasses were already off.

"Joseph," the Doomer hissed. His Brooklynese voice had always been a tense whisper, like a thin, punctured tire releasing air in disheartening spurts.

"Is that your voice on this tape...?"

"Yes, Brother," I quivered.

"Did you play this tape just now over the P.A. System, Joseph . . . ?"

"N-n-no, Brother."

"But did you make this tape, Joseph?"

"Well, that is my voi-voi — I made the tape for a friend, sir."

The Doomer sat back, squinting, pressing fingertips together.

"And who is this friend of yours, Joseph . . . ? Who played this tape just now from my office . . . ? Will you tell me that?"

My spine was trickling southward while my hair and socks curled in and out, up and down. I was ready to faint.

"N-n-no, Brother."

"No?"

"Well, I mean, I could tell you whose tape it is, but I have no idea if he was the one who played it just now."

The Vice-Principal paused.

"Well, that's good. Because if you *had* told me, Joseph, I would have expelled you on the spot."

My mouth must have fallen open. Brother Patrick... smiled!!

"Now let me tell you something else . . . That is a very funny tape!!"

I thought I was in "The Twilight Zone", or hearing things at least, until the Doomer leaned forward.

"It's all right. Sit down."

I sat. I needed to sit.

"I had no idea you were so funny, Joseph... For four years, you've tried to get a theatre department started here, and although we couldn't afford it, now I know why you kept trying. You're quite talented. You ought to try Show Business as a profession."

A week before graduating, I was hearing my true vocation spelled out for me from the most unlikely source imaginable, under the strangest of circumstances.

Of course, I knew I'd always wanted that for myself, but never dreamt I'd be hearing encouragement from the notoriously strict commandant of this all-boy military high school.

That wasn't all the encouragement I got either.

After being dismissed by Brother Patrick, a body of fellow students starting lunch period broke out into spontaneous applause.

Other teachers took me aside to advise pretty much the same thing that the Doomer did.

With this, my fate was irrevocably sealed. Even my family had to reluctantly agree with the Doomer's surprise recommendation and my own heartfelt decision.

So Show Biz it would be.

And from the late 19th century to date, I'm the only alumnus La-Salle Institute of Troy, New York has ever listed in their rolls as a professional actor.

Chapter 4:
Other Celebrities I Have Known and Loved Meeting
(And I'll make this a short chapter, I promise.)

*B*efore I continue explaining my development as a voice actor, I feel like recounting some star-sightings I experienced while growing up in New York State's Tri-City area, or Capital District, or Metroland, as we've called it from time to time. (Albany, in case you didn't know, is the capital. That's pronounced: ALL-buh-nee, for those of you who have never landed at its dinky, intentionally dwarfed "International" airport. And even then, the flight attendants say "Al-BANNY." But it does exist, really.)

Anyway, in swingin' upstate New York State, home of the Abominably Snowbound, there were by geographical and societal definition almost no opportunities to meet anybody famous. But the encounters I experienced as a kid were all funny ones somehow.

At a local fair, my Dad took me to see a world-class ventriloquist, the late Paul Winchell. I watched his TV show regularly and adored not only his terrific sense of humor, but his amazing expertise at developing a separate reality for his wooden friends to expand their world of activities. (They flew kites, they made breakfast, they *swam*, for corn's sake!!) I couldn't have been older than six. Dad took me for a walk to find him (!!) and we did (!!); he was rehearsing with Jerry Mahoney outside a gazebo encircled by a white corral fence.

Dad said, "There he is. Call him over."

So I did, probably saying something like, "Hey!! Paul Winchell!! C'mere!!"

Amused, he did walk over to us, with Jerry on his arm. Aside from asking "Where's Knucklehead Smiff?", I can't recall what was actually said, but Dad says I was doing my puerile parodies for him the way a kid unselfconsciously does when he feels like it. I recollect Winch chuckling at my simple shenanigans, and getting an earful of encouragement from his arboreal alter ego, and really digging his live show later even more than I'd anticipated!! He was as nice as he could be to me.

Years later, my first Hollywood voice-over (v/o) agent was his as well. He'd become Dick Dastardly and other popular cartoon characters since we'd last met.

But I didn't mention our past encounter because this reunion was under much less happy circumstances: it was the week he'd heard that some storage facility had bulk-erased his video legacy following a dispute over his bill. He was heartsick over this ultimate vandalism, I hear, for the rest of his life. Business versus Art. Winch sued and won, and lost anyway. Was any artist ever treated worse? I might've brought a cannon to court.

Lovable lunk Joe E. Ross, who also rounded out his career in animation, attended the same annual event a couple-or-few years later. From the burlesque stage, he rose to fame as Sgt. Ritzik on "The Phil Silvers Show" (aka "You'll Never Get Rich" & "Sgt. —" aw, you know.) and TV stardom for two seasons on "Car 54, Where Are You?", both Nat Hiken shows. I wasn't exactly enamored of Mr. Ross, but like most of America in the early '60s, I found drollness in his coarse, cheery enthusiasm as Officer Gunther Toody.

Other Celebrities I Have Known and Loved Meeting   21

On that fateful day he came to the Saratoga Racetrack, in order to meet this visiting luminary, one had to stand and shuffle slowly forward in a long, long line on a hot, hot day. Well, he was that year's main attraction, and I was young, so stand and shuffle I did, along with my Dad. And as everyone sweltered, human aromas merging with equine, we drew ever closer, baby-stepping dutifully . . .

Then, I could hear, only faintly at first, the phrase "Ooh!! Ooh!!" being repeated in approximately twenty-second intervals. "Ooh!! Ooh . . . !! . . . Ooh!! Ooh . . . !!"

And I noted with growing concern that the closer I got, the louder the ooh-oohs got. Maybe the sun was getting to me. Finally, I reached welcome shade. Though here the ooh-oohs were deafening, almost threatening!! "Ooh!! Ooh!! — Ooh!! Ooh . . . !!" The tension was bearable for most of his Tri-Cities fans moving nearer, ever nearer, ever faster!!

"Oomp-Oomp!! Oomp-Oomp!!" my heart raced.

Then, lo and behold, in costume as Toody, but sporting sunglasses and sipping an enviably large iced tea through a straw as he lounged in a lounge chair, the one and only, horizontal Joe E. Ross loomed into view!! He and his handlers were really scooting the folks along now. The next race was about to begin, in which case we'd have to just stand and wait, the inexorable shufflers halted, ooh-ooh-less, as he watched the Sport of Kings.

But all of a sudden, it was my turn to meet him!!

Dad pushed me forward. I didn't know what to say.

"Tell him to say ooh-ooh," suggested helpful Dad.

And I did. And I got my own personal dose of it, a noncommittal but anti-climactically hilarious "Ooh!! Ooh!!"

Then he turned to one of his guys and said "Okay. That's enough for now," slurped his last sip, got up and left, his back drenched in summer dew.

"Wow!!" I thought. "I got his last Ooh-ooh!!"

For a half-hour at least, I betcha.

This next story isn't about a voice actor, but I think it's worthy of inclusion here because it was a rare opportunity to talk to a cultural champion — on a good, old-fashioned pay phone!! If you're a comic book fan, you'll especially enjoy this, I'm sure.

It happened on a trip to New York City. Dad hauled me and Gary Rafferty, my boyhood chum from our hometown of Troy, New York. I was a Yankees fan, Dad liked the White Sox, and Gary liked neither team, so off we all went to see New York play Chicago.

But Gary and I had another sojourn in mind.

We tried to see if we could tour the new Marvel Comics offices, à la *Mad* magazine. Dad got us to the address, but we were told no such tour existed. As we were leaving, Gary spotted a dapper, bearded fella in a jazzy, short-brimmed lid, whistling merrily as he got out of the elevator. This was Stan Lee, we realized, — Who else could be that happy coming out of that building?! — but he was gone before we could near him, absorbed by the bustling throng without.

I've met and talked to Stan several times since then, mostly at the San Diego Comics Convention: a real nice guy, very easy to approach.

But Gary and I weren't done exploring yet. Stan was the writer, but then there were some favorite Marvel artists to investigate, like Steve Ditko, co-creator and artist of Marvel Comics' Spider-Man, whose exploits were only about a year old back then. (The first issue I ever read was # 6.)

Mr. Ditko had already begun to develop a reputation as a reclusive genius, shunning most interviews and certainly photographers. But Gary and I lucked out somehow . . . I wrote the following piece for Ditko Looked Up (website "ditko.comics.org") awhile back, and, hoping you'll forgive a few redundancies, now reprint it here.

I was ten years old when Spidey first hit the stands. I'd already gotten hooked on the Marvel monster stuff that preceded him. I even remember thinking, "Hey, this *Amazing Fantasy* comic is cool!! A whole book drawn by my favorite guy!!" Wow, what that became . . .

24 "That's _Still_ Not All, Folks!!"

So, a year or so later (circa *Amazing Spider-Man* # 11 or 12), my Dad took me and a friend to see a ball game. But our young minds strayed elsewhere . . .

We found Steve Ditko's name in the phone book (!!?!) and promptly called him.

He answered. He sounded busy.

But we stammered and effused about his work as best we could and, to our shared disbelief, were granted a brief conversation with him!!

We asked how he liked doing Spidey; he was cool enough to reply, "I hope Stan will let me develop the stories more." Old news now, but, hey, in those days, this was a scoop!!

We asked how he thought up that cool costume. He said, proudly, "That's my job."

We told him what our favorite stories were (#s 2, 3 & 4) and praised the villains. My buddy said he loved the friction with JJJ too.

"Thanks..."

(Uh-oh!! He's starting to sound bored!!) We were already forgetting the rest of what we wanted to ask!!

I then asked him how old he was: a typical kid question. There was a long pause.

"How old do you think I should be?" he asked back.

We waffled some more, instantly embarrassed, and I said, "Twenty? Thirty . . . ?"

"Better stop there," he said, adding (something like) "Go back to twenty," very wryly.

And before we could ask if we could visit him at his studio, he finished with, "And I gotta go back to work to keep kids like you happy."

That comment alone was almost worth not visiting him, in retrospect.

And my friend and I have relived this brief brush with His Mysterious Highness often enough to remember it practically verbatim.

What's a memory like *that* worth?

To round off this story, though I've never voiced as many superhero cartoons as I would've liked, for the first version of Spidey's second game, I did manage to land the dual role of Dr. Connors and The Lizard, — the villain of *Amazing Spider-Man* # 6!! Love those beautiful karmic cycles!! (And recently, in another Spidey game, I played the beloved, humorless Doctor Octopus, aka Doc Ock!!)

Dad was back for the next celebrity sighting, on that same trip to Manhattan, after the Yankees game.

In front of some hotel, I spotted actor Norman Fell, many years previous to his "Three's Company" co-star status. But I liked his dust-dry, deadpan deliveries in drama and comedy alike. I always read credits on everything I watched, so I knew who he was anyway.

"Look, Dad!! There's Norman Fell!!" I chirruped.

"Who?"

After an quick explanation, I broke away just long enough to ask the man if he was indeed Norman Fell. His response was gratifying, and rather gratified as well.

"Kid," he growled, "You're the first person who ever knew my name!!" We both laughed, though I thought that must have been an exaggeration.

"You want my autograph? I haven't got a pen," he continued.

"Me neither," I informed him. We both laughed again and he tousled my hair. Like I was a little kid or somethin'.

"Well, maybe next time!!" he concluded, sending me back to my puzzled father.

"Who'd ya say that was?"

"Norman Fell."

Other Celebrities I Have Known and Loved Meeting

"Oh . . . Yeah. Right."

Ever since then, I kept an eye open for character actors, and was rewarded often once I got to Hollywood. Though I allowed no more tousling.

Norman fell into my line of vision again, when I was teamed with him for the celebrity "Family Feud" years later. And this time there was nothing to prevent me from reminding him of our initial meeting.

So I said, "Hey, Norman Fell, remember me? I was the kid you once told was the first person ever to recognize you by name!!"

And he said, "Oh . . . Yeah. Right."

How my heart sang.

Gary also turned me on to Bob and Ray, who by the late '60s were being marketed in a hard rock format (!!) called "The Music Factory."

We devised another plan to invade New York City, posing as (no kidding, now) "reporters" who wished to interview them. And we left Dad home this time.

They agreed, and when we met Bob in his office, he called Ray in to, we now think, get a kick outta these two high-schoolers and their keen, teen handheld reel-to-reel tape recorder. But they were gentlemen and played along with us for at least a half-hour.

That tape, darn it, has since vanished, but I can tell you we asked if Webley Webster was supposed to have teeth or not, and if Ray had appeared as a dance extra in the Van Johnson-Esther Williams effort *Thrill of a Romance*. He denied this vehemently (even after I showed him the photo) and Bob started kidding him about it — subtly, of course. I'd like to think Bob kept it up after that for at least a year.

Leaving the Graybar Building, we nervy kids were only sorry we hadn't mentioned any embarrassing moments that Ray could razz Bob about!!

Gary and I still enjoy long phone talks, mostly revolving around old movies and TV, and still share about 88 laughs per call.

But enough about other people. Here's more about me . . .

Chapter 5:
I Get into Theatre – and Vice Versa

I was a freshman at Siena College at sixteen and immediately went into radio, pitching and landing a weekly half-hour show I wrote and directed and called "Put-On." This was a hippie-epoch combination of mind-games with a heavy Bob and Ray influence, immodestly peopled by only myself and my penchant for verbal multi-tasking.

A striking personality named Ron Vawter heard this program and rushed to introduce me to the Theatre Department, where I began to flourish (thanks, of course, to my understanding and application of generous portions of tasty Ham). Ron and I co-starred in several local productions, some of which he also directed.

Ron, by the way, went on to become a highly-regarded actor and director of the NYC Underground Theatre scene, before popping up in films like *sex, lies and videotape*, *The Silence of the Lambs* and *Philadelphia*. His sudden and most untimely demise in 1994 was an awful shock. As my theatre mentor and friend, I miss him a lot.

During the run of sixty-odd plays and showcases in which I've participated since the age of fifteen, I'm happy to say I apparently achieved my goal right off the bat. In my very first college role as the religious hypocrite John Tetzel in John Osborne's *Luther*, I was praised in local reviews as an actor. They reported that I managed to tread the tricky tightrope between the character's lightest and darkest sides and emerge as a standout amongst the cast. (One of the reviewers gave me three paragraphs!!)

I was seventeen and I knew what I was doing, but only because I'd done my homework. Or should I say "hamwork."

And before I knew it (but after I planned it), I started specializing in villains.

In *The Trial*, which was performed in the round, I had the part of a snide Deputy Bank Director. It wasn't a very noticeable role until one night, holding a prop telephone, I tripped down the steps and all 300-plus pounds of me went skidding on my stomach straight to Center Stage. I got up, brushed myself off, handed the phone to "Joseph K" (Ron) and delivered my line, "It's for you — " adding, ad lib, "Long distance . . . " I don't think Kafka would've approved. Ron didn't. But the audience lost it, grateful for a laugh in the middle of such foreboding modern melodrama.

I meandered through *Fortune and Men's Eyes* as a surly, gastrically-challenged prison screw. One of the actors in it not-so-jokingly threatened to beat me up for being too realistically anti-gay!! (I'm pretty sure he was using the Method.)

Then I switched colleges to major in Theatre and did four plays in two semesters.

In Stephen Vincent Benet's *The Devil and Daniel Webster*, the charming, malicious Mr. Scratch tempts and misleads a farmer to his near-doom. All these roles offered subtle but juicy bad-guy parts, and I dug into all of them with gusto (which is as good as spicy mustard with you-know-what). In the last of these mentioned, maybe I should also mention that I was the only adult in a student project I also directed at a local orphanage. Yeah, some villain.

In Elaine May's *Adaptation*, I was the Male Player, a multi-character role in which I not only played the hero's father, but a motivational speaker, for which I was encouraged to do an impression, that of George C. Scott. A hammy George C. Scott. (— but not as hammily as himself in one of the best-balanced Ham-o-ramas ever committed to film, *Dr. Strangelove*.)

As the sly, asthmatic Marquis deSade (Why would I lie?) in a staging of the mad *Marat/Sade* (Ron Vawter played Marat, FYI), I was steered away from Ham for once, although we all played in a heightened stage style of the past.

But it was as Zanni, a dippy, doddering centenarian in the Commedia del Arte classic *The Three Cuckolds* that I had the most fun. In this show, much dialogue and character-sculpture was improvised by everyone, as the style traditionally dictates. In this show, I did my own latex old-age makeup, wore a pith helmet and dragged behind me a beribboned saucepot I called "Kitty."

Next thing I knew, the students were talking about awards. I had to ask what was going on: A friend told me I'd just broken the record for the department's annual acting nominations, scoring in three out of four categories!! And a couple of weeks later, I won for Zanni, their Best Supporting Actor in a Major Production!!

I did not give a tearful, stammering speech, thanking dozens. Though I was ecstatic and hammily humble.

That summer, some of us formed a troupe that was a children's improvisational touring company called PlayPeople. Lotsa fun. Kids are the most honest audiences.

Nighttimes, we also presented the stage version of Joseph Heller's *Catch-22* for adult audiences, both under the direction of future Jeopardy Super-Champion Bob Verini. More hopping in and out of characters was in order, and it was a good, fun learning experience for us all.

The best story from this stint happened when, after we did Act I of the play in rustic Slingerlands, New York, the audience (whom we outnumbered by two or three) applauded enthusiastically. We took our intermission break, and ten minutes later, were two or three minutes into Act II when we slowly realized that the entire house had gone home, thinking the play was over!! At which point, we threw a party and did most of Act II anyway. And laughed all the way home.

I also participated in other schools' productions. In Russell Sage College's presentation of Brecht's *The Caucasian Chalk Circle*, I played the redoubtable but wise judge Azdak (still one of my favorite roles).

I also got the lead in Alfred Jarry's *Ubu Roi* (and did part two, *Ubu in Chains*, decades later in L.A., which might make me the only actor alive who's done both halves of this absurdist landmark).

In *Adrienne LeCouvreur*, I was le Abbé deChauzeil, the red herring in an 18th-Century murder mystery. (Close enough to "Burke's Law," I guess.)

Samuel Beckett's *Krapp's Last Tape* is a one-man vignette which I slapped together ("directed myself" is the euphemism), and in the same author's *Waiting for Godot*, also at Russell Sage, I cracked the Hambone whip as Pozzo (a role I reprised in NYC to better reviews).

All this was in a three-year period, from 1969 to '72.

Man!! Where did I find the energy?!

The same year I graduated from high school, I did my first commercial, a TV spot for Blue Cross/Blue Shield. I played a sarcastic car mechanic. So this was the job that brought me my first paycheck for "Show Biz" (sixty-five bucks — even my Dad was impressed).

To this day, however, I not only don't know a thing about cars, still don't drive, and never have. And one reason is because I know how bad I am at it. You should thank me for staying off the road. And in the meantime, keep paying for your car, your insurance, your gas . . .

Taxi!!

By the end of the semester at a second university, I found myself in an unexpected academic pickle. A tenured professor asked me to be in his production of *Mary Stewart* (again as the villain, the brutal Lord

Bothwell). Then, another tenured academician requested my services for *The Wizard of Oz* (as either the Cowardly Lion or the Wizard). To my delight, this show was to tour Russia!!

But to my horror, it was scheduled concurrently with the other show!! I felt terrific that I was in demand, but knowing I couldn't do both, I approached both these teacher/directors and pled my case. The response from each of them was an adamant insistence that I refuse the other offer — or else I couldn't take their class next year, both of which were required for my degree!!

I went to the head of the department. Knowing my diploma was at stake, he said he sympathized with me but flatly refused to get involved.

All three of these educators were tenured, by the way. They certainly taught me more than my tuition covered.

Funny. I can't seem to recall the name of that college. (Oh, well. It's not important.)

Anyway, unable to solve this scholastic dilemma myself, I opted to do neither show and simply left the premises. As a result, I never did get my degree.

But, boy, was I popular!!

Chapter 6:
The Big Apple and the Worm

So I opted for Plan B and took off for the place where actors in theatre, even Hams, must go if they want to become professionals. I was twenty years old and itching to see if I could get into a Broadway show. And it was only a hundred-and-fifty miles away!!

I enjoyed dozens of interesting and worthwhile experiences amidst my fifteen-year theatrical period, but Broadway remained elusive.

In New York City for five hard years (circa 1973-'78), I was a starving actor. I proceed to prove the adage by dwindling from about 250 to 185 pounds in my first year!! (Don't worry. I gained it all back. Then lost it again.)

The New York Theatre Scene was more densely populated than the student lounge, naturally, and almost as fiercely competitive, yet I managed to get to work right away — though I always had to supplement my eager, non-Equity salaries with some nine-to-five job or another. I programmed a prehistoric computer for an insurance company, sliced lox paper-thin and cut giant wheels of Parmesan in a cheese shop, and even apprenticed as a diamond-cutter!! (Good thing I always had a steady hand.)

I was never lucky enough to catch hold of the real-life Catch-22 of being able to join a union — any union — by getting into a union show, though I tried and tried again to rise above the steamy drudgery of cattle-call auditions.

So, meanwhile, I worked and played in several classical and original works and plays Off-, Off-Off-, and way Off-Broadway, including *Murder in the Cathedral* (Ham), *A Streetcar Named Desire* (non-Ham), *The Playboy of the Western World* (both), and *Tartuffe* (the title role: one huge, shameless, though organic, overstuffed Ham).

In the film *The Goodbye Girl*, Richard Dreyfuss's character essays a gay Richard III in a real-life theatre called The Open Space. Three or four years earlier, I played a swishy stage manager in *The Last Christians*, an original play produced in real life at the same place!! Interesting, huh? (Ya had to be there, I guess.)

Maybe a better anecdote would be my encounter with one of my aforementioned heroes of Ham, the verbal virtuoso Hans Conried, one of whose greatest character creations was himself. (Don't forget Captain Hook and Snidely Whiplash!!)

In the winter of '76, my eccentric mentor-figure was rehearsing something called *Something Old, Something New* at the Morosco on Broadway (which ran for one entire performance). He was surprisingly tall in his greatcoat and beret, and utterly unmistakable to me as he glided towards me down 5th Avenue one chilly afternoon.

I stood in his way on the sidewalk and babbled something like, "Oh, gosh, Mr. Conried!! I've always wanted to meet you!! I'm probably your greatest fan!! I love everything you've ever done!!"

To which he replied with practiced eyebrow-arch-and-sniff, "Oh, rrrreally . . . !!" and a mask-dropping smirk.

It was pure Conried, and I loved it.

And he did it 'cause he knew I'd love it.

And as he pushed off, his parting smile let me see how much he loved it too.

That is premium Ham, folks: one who knew another Ham when he saw him, and one who could kid his own ego just to get a laugh!!

(Or maybe his show had opened the night before . . . ?)

Another celebrity anecdote? Sure!!

When Joe Papp was doing Shakespeare in the Park (Central, of course), I tried like hell to get an audition, but they were done with that.

In the meantime, sometimes, when I was able, I'd watch PBS's "The Electric Company," a wonderful show that encouraged pre-teens to read — but with a cast to die for: Rita Moreno, occasionally Bill Cosby, and six or seven other fine, versatile and near-Ham performers, including a young legend-to-be, who was also in Papp's SITP shows.

To cut to the chase, one day an old fella fainted right in front of a West Side movie house, and me, at high noon. I reached down for his arm. Another hand reached for his other arm, the hand of Morgan Freeman. I recognized him instantly and again babbled praise at him. I think I surprised the gracious good Samaritan with my knowledge of his budding career. To this day, I only wish he'd ham it up a little more, as he did on that kids' show. Too much dignity is his problem!! (But he earned it.)

An exciting though incomplete chapter from my New York days was being briefly involved in what was to be a Great White Way revival of *Of Thee I Sing* which was being prepared by the legendary George Abbott!!

But, alas, the money fell through. Oh, well. No regrets. At least I was in his presence for awhile, and the experience lasted a good two weeks, which was the average run of my shows anyway.

Another celebrity meeting that was a little more frightening was while I was doing *Streetcar*.

The production was bootleg, meaning we weren't paying for the rights, and none of were paid either. Rest assured, knowing these facts beforehand didn't stop us from putting it on. I was playing the naïve Mitch, the role for which Karl Malden won the Oscar in 1951.

Well, with my luck, what do you think happened?

That's right: Tennessee Williams himself showed up!! We were sure he was there to shut us down!! But instead, the legendary playwright sat through the whole thing and told the company, after a comically mild rebuke, that he enjoyed it enough to let us finish our run. We were thankful to be spared his authorial wrath. He even congratulated us for getting the New Orleans accents right!! (Ever see the movie? Mr. Malden doesn't have one.)

It was also during this show's run that, one night walking home after the curtain, I saved myself from gang violence, merely by doing an impression — my impression of an enraged, penniless actor who was ready to hurl them all into moving traffic if they got to within six feet of me!!

Strangely, I don't get many calls for that one anymore.

I also did my first v/o job around this time, though I wouldn't do another for years. That's okay. It *ran* for years, a sappy computer-dating service spot featuring some of the homeliest creatures on Earth. It ran for *nine* years, and if you've guessed by now that I never got Residual One for it, you're right: it was a buyout (one-time payment).

But I sure dated a lot!!

At this time, too, in dim and smoky NYC comedy clubs, I watched, spellbound, the routines of, among others, the fascinating Andy Kaufman. And I saw *Lemmings* with John Belushi. Significantly, perhaps, they both were revered for one fantastic singing impression each: Kaufman - Elvis Presley; Belushi - Joe Cocker. Soon, like the rest of the country, I was slavishly following their inspired small-screen antics as well, and working on my Richie Havens. (Rent *Woodstock* to find out who that is.)

But stand-up and sketch-shows were their calling, and I was but a pale, quaking thing within the shadows of their ill-fated but well-earned fame, still flailing around onstage in "legit" stuff. Only infrequently did I dare to tenderly test my toes in the comedy mainstream's waters.

It took a cruel twist of fate to land me in another major city and force me to dive headlong into the world of stand-up.

This harsh happenstance occurred when I was between apartments in Manhattan and sub-letting one from an actor acquaintance.

What happened was: I was burgled by a big-time outfit that used a moving van and a team of uniformed, fake moving-man thieves!! The police later told me that these misguided souls specialized in wiping people out of *all* their possessions, not to mention their dreams. So, yes, they heartlessly removed absolutely everything tangible that belonged to me, — and the acquaintance.

Well, he wasn't much of a friend; the news of our mutual misfortune moved him to landlord it over me, blaming blameless me for the Moving Van Gang's criminal expertise.

"I know I locked that door before I left for work!!" was my logical defense.

But he didn't wanna hear logic. He demanded total recompense from yours truly.

And although I heartily disagreed with his judgment, I paid him what I could (which was, as Justice would have it, very little), and was myself moved to move to Massachusetts at the invitation of a much truer pal, good ol' Gary Rafferty.

Then things got really interesting. And by that I mean "successful" and — even better — "fun"!! (For a change.)

Chapter 7:
The Boston Tee-Hee Party

Okay, I hereby promise not to pun too much henceforth, but this chapter's title fits really well.

It was very much a party in BeanTown, where I finally tried stand-up. Not only was I lucky enough to be included in the roster of some excellent and soon-to-be-famous comedy stars, but also used that springboard to leap back into radio, and consequently, cross-country.

When I arrived in late '77, Gary picked up where Ron and other good friends left off, urging me to try my hand at live comedy at a year-old place downtown called The Comedy Connection.

This scared me more than a little, but I was game. I worked up ten minutes and auditioned for it. My fledgling act was comprised of sarcastic little tributes to "The Andy Griffith Show," "Rocky and His Friends" (aka "The Bullwinkle Show"), and "The Honeymooners."

Eschewing props, costumes and makeups, I did employ a musical instrument with which I had practiced many long, tedious hours of sweat and tears, and yes, blood too. Man, it took me months to perfect the kazoo. Oh, sure, its color has faded and it's a bit rusty, but as I look at it now, I'm overcome with emotion — the emotion of embarrassment. I think I'll throw the damn thing away. Rust — Yecch.

And despite my skimpy experience, I lucked out. I was soon mak-

42 "That's _Still_ Not All, Folks!!"

ing a little money at being an impressionist, and within months, added to my stage time and became one of the most popular acts in Boston's burgeoning, soon-to-be-legendary stand-up comedy scene of the late '70s and '80s.

It wasn't about the money, believe me. But if you did enough gigs, a little piled up in the long run.

The stand-up scene was terrific fun, and I wouldn't trade my memories or experiences on the road for anything, except ones involving both Hillary Duff and Cool Whip Lite.

I don't mean to kid about it. The gags just sorta bubble up to the surface whenever I recall those wonderful salad years. In Boston, of course, it was bean salad.

I worked in all three of the major clubs in town. (So make that a three-bean salad, okay?) There were, in order of my exposure to them, the Comedy Connection (Thank you, Bil Downes and Paul Barclay, for my first paid gigs), the Ding Ho (Thank you, Chung Lee, for all that great, free Chinese food!!) and Nick's Lounge. And later, Stitches, Play It Again Sam's, and a smattering of other rooms emerged. But it really didn't smatter where we worked. We were like a big, happy family. Mostly guys. A big, happy, drunken, drugged-out, womanizing family.

All kidding aside, — Well, most kidding aside, life-long friendships did grow and prosper, there was always laughter in the air, and consequently, very few accusations of actual murder were ever proven.

Now all kidding aside, an hilarious handful of present-day comedy greats emerged from this place not long afterward: rock-solid, stone-faced Steven Wright (with whom I used to work at the MIT CoOp (we were both "trouble-shooters" [??]); Bobcat Goldthwait (I think he pronounces it "Goal-waith"); Paula Poundstone (whom I once saw perform in a skirt); political thorns Barry Crimmins (a sincere soul who also booked acts for the legendary "Ding") and Jim Morris (His Ronald Reagan was the best when it counted most); absurdist Ron Lynch (formerly of Bob and Ron, whose Sunday night showcase was my first. He's now keeping very busy in L.A.); a young, chain-smoking Denis Leary; nutty but nice Kevin Meaney; lewd and uproarious Lenny Clarke; keen, kinetic Tom Kenny (aka SpongeBob SquarePants); — even a couple o' guys who *aren't* Irish!!

Oh, and, uh, Jay Leno... Believe me now?

Actually, Jay was working in and out of Boston years before our club scene began. We newcomers adored him just for getting knocked out by a flying beer bottle at a strip joint one night (which resulted in a net being strung over the stage area — um, so I've heard). But I understand he was very helpful getting a club or two started before he left. Most memorably for me, he asked me to be the announcer on his very first (I think) TV show, a 60-minute local comedy special, "The First Boston Driver's Test."

(More on Jay after I hit L.A.)

That special was for WSBK, where we eventually all had fun. Martin Olson (and friends) wrote and produced "The Lenny Clarke Show" there in the early '80s.

Lenny ruled the roost at that time, having the hottest Saturday night show in town for as long as he was there.

On Channel 38, he hosted schlocky movies with wacky wraparounds. This was real TV, kiddoes, and real funny to boot. Every week Lenny unleashed his typically wild-eyed, frenetic rap; conducted crazy character interviews and starred in skits with top local comics and friends like Mike Donovan, Mike McDonald, Don Gavin and Steve Sweeney.

And there were fake commercials. I was asked to write and performed two of these myself: one pastiche of a long-running classical music package touted by a jaded, insulting snob (Ham and typecasting); and an insurance spot offering eternal coverage by "Old Nick" himself. (This one featured some neat special effects at the end: horns seemed to grow right up out of my skull!!) (More typecasting.)

Lenny is now a popular character actor with many roles and three or four TV series to his credit.

Gary and I pitched Channel 38 a similar concept only months before Lenny's show debuted, in which I played a would-be scary late-night horror movie host named Konrad. It's just as well they passed; Lenny and Martin's show was much wider in scope, imagination, and budget.

A colorful character, nice guy and musical merry-maker named Chance Langton also provided me with much work. He'd get big yocks by imitating Johnny Cash on acid: "Ah see the train a-comin'" — then he'd widen freaked-out eyes and just collapse. Or he'd lay horizontally across a barstool and croon "I did it Sideways . . . " I kinda miss this wry guy.

A real good buddy to me was and still is one Martin Olson (formerly known as E. Martin Olson). A talented musician, composer, scenarist and comediturge, he helped shape and write some of a lot of new comics' earliest stage pieces, least memorably perhaps something for me that he called "Mayberry LSD." (Can you guess the premise?)

We still write together from time to time, and I predict that one day his name will be known far and wide. Because today, Martin bought a machine gun. (He also has a lovely family . . . of hammerhead sharks. — But they're lovely!!)

I'd have to say the audiences seemed to be having more fun back then, too, especially the "regulars" (people who showed up and sat at the same tables every Thursday night). In retrospect, that's the best way I can put it. Maybe because it was relatively new to all of us. Or maybe they just drank more.

We'd occasionally get a celeb in the audience, in town to do a show or whatever.

I remember the late actor Richard Jordan and his date helping me out with a much-needed ride to a crosstown gig opening for singer Phoebe Snow — in their limo.

We '80s Boston Comics hobnobbed with rock musicians and pro wrestlers like "Rowdy Roddy" Piper and George "the Animal" Steele (not too closely. My hobs have been nobbed enough, thanks).

Garrulous gent Orson Bean told me a true story at the bar about how he once tried to talk a tailor into selling him a pocket hanky on display in his window, one which was embroidered, "Your Name Here." (The tailor didn't get it.)

Sometimes the stars worked with us: I worked with Bean, and later with malaprop-meister Norm Crosby at the Connection. Surefire sharpie Elayne Boosler came in and did an hour; I watched the whole thing, awed by her ingenuity and audience command.

And I remember when a bunch of us performed at Carly Simon's club on Nantucket, where we sat with —

Oh, you'd like to see a few samples from my act? Okay.

Time once again for "Bad Casting — all the right actors in all the wrong but oddly appropriate roles."

Here's a scene you don't remember from *The Ten Commandments*, with Charlton Heston as Moses . . .

CHARLTON HESTON: O Mighty Pharaoh!! — In the name of the Great Jehovah, unless you set my people free, yet another plague shall be visited upon you . . . and all your people . . . !!

RODNEY DANGERFIELD: Hey, come on, lighten up, willya, Moses?! Oh, I tell ya, Pharaoh don't get no respect. No respect at all. You're up there on the mountain with the burnin' bush — We're down here in rough shape!! Why don't you and your plagues take a forty-year hike off a short pier? First it's the boils, then the flies, the bats, the frogs, the locusts — Do me a favor, willya? *Make up your mind!!* Talk about your God of vengeance — This is like a weekend with my wife!!

I offered Shakespeare, done by . . .

SLIM PICKENS *(as Hamlet)*: Wal, *to* be or not to be. *That's* a good question. Whether 'tis nobler in the *mind* to suffer th' slings an' arrows o' outrageous fortune, an' — Look out, Ophelia!! Them thar's *fire arrows!! (Getting one in the shoulder.)* Well, shoot. *(Snaps it off.)* How's about we jus' start a-sword-fahtin'?

— and . . .

ARCHIE BUNKER as **ROMEO**: Hey, Mercutio there . . . !! Hey, g'wan, you jest at scars that never felt a wound, haah? Oh yeah? Well, *(Bronx cheer)* to you too . . . Hey, wait a minute here. What's all that soft stuff breakin' t'rough the window up there . . . ? Aw, Jeeze, it's that Juliet I met at that party the other night!! Wait a minute here, I think she's gonna talk!!

EDITH BUNKER as **JULIET**: Oh, Romeo, Romeo, wherefore art thou, Romeo? Oh!! Deny thy *father* — *(Very high pitched trill.)* Yeah-h-h!! And refuse thy name!! After all, that which we call a rose by any other name still . . . smells nice . . . Doesn't it?

ARCHIE BUNKER as **ROMEO**: Aw, jeeze. She's verily a dingbat!! Hey, Mercutio!! Wait up there, haahh?!

Bardwise, I also submitted Arnold Schwarzenegger as a much more decisive (Uzi-toting) Hamlet, and Joe Pesci as a much less subtle Richard III. (More about this good fella later, believe it or not.)

For the next seven years or so, I was actually in demand as an impressionist, or "facsimiloquist" (another word I've coined to make me seem more important). To my gratification and great relief, audiences rather loved my tight little spins on Jackie Gleason and Art Carney as Ralph Kramden and Ed Norton, whom I recreated in a number of ways. (I know you know who played who. Just giving credit where it's due.)

Looking more like "the Great One" than anyone else I did, I was kinda stuck with doing him for a long time. And while I soaked up the kudos, the irony is that I didn't and still don't admire Gleason very much personally. I thought he was a superb and very innovative talent, but behind the scenes, I came to discover that he was dishearteningly unprofessional.

And I know for a fact that I've rehearsed his stuff more than he ever did!!

It's just too bad for all of us that, from beginning to end, he seemed to love several things more than comedy.

O, media pioneer!! I wonder how I'd have done things in his place?

But ya know what? If I had my choice of generations, I'd I think I'd have preferred making silent film comedies instead. No, I'm not kidding. I've always had a special love, and a strong affinity for non-verbal physical comedy. Yes, I've seen and studied as much of that as I could too. Charlie Chaplin, Buster Keaton, Harold Lloyd — Voiceless or not, they were the *first* recorded pioneers!!

But I stayed in the present, and concentrated on my greatest strength, hammering away at many personal favorites in my act, which was mostly comprised of more playful "Bad Casting":

Don Knotts became Abra-Ham Lincoln, delivering the Gettysburgh Address a little too officiously.

The Marx Brothers starred in *2001: a Space Odyssey*, with Groucho as HAL the computer.

Orson Welles sheepishly admitted he was "coo-coo for Cocoa Puffs," while an irritated Marlon Brando filled in for the Trix rabbit, scattering children and cereal alike.

Vincent Price uncharacteristically slung lead as either a Western gunslinger or Dirty Harry.

Remember "Perry Mason"? I offered club patrons Raymond Burr's thoughtful, somber rendition of "Wild Thing," complete with glottal inhalations and windmill-armed air-guitar riffs punctuating the lyrics.

Don Rickles' Charlie Brown reversed the loser image once and for all, verbally spanking all his playmates.

Walter Matthau and Jack Lemmon squabbled over who would go town for supplies as The Lone Ranger and Tonto.

Peter Lorre, toy switchblade in hand, purred and bellowed the Rolling Stones' "Satisfaction" to front-row girls cringing behind their Stingers.

Dustin Hoffman's *Rain Man* later became my opening stand-up act, complimenting his "very sparkly, very twinkly" audience and counting swizzle sticks.

Woody Allen was still getting nowhere with women as Dr. Hannibal Lecter.

I imagined Jack Nicholson as Eddie Haskell putting a sly make on "Juuune" Cleaver. "Pearls and high heels in the kitchen? You hot ticket, you!!" (Set-up by John Byner.)

And other punishing routines that somehow worked.

(Hmm. Maybe I oughtta revive that act someday...)

I thought it was somewhat cool to perform entire-cast set pieces like "Star Trek," wherein everyone aboard faced annihilation while coping with a cosmic knock-knock joke.

I retraced Dorothy's steps in fear and loathing of *The Wizard of Oz* and all its weird denizens, avoiding talking apple trees and the Munchkin Coroner — though I'd also do Bert Lahr's unforgettable solo as verbatim as possible (or let Rod Steiger take a whack at it).

At about this point in my act, I would tend to spritz. My advice to any heavyweight person in a jacket and tie under hot lights in a small room is to expect this physiological phenomenon to occur.

It's not bad enough that I have to avoid strong lights because my eyes lack the normal human amount of natural UV protection, — No, I also hadda be a spritzer!!

Old Faithful's got nothin' on me!! I had to sell umbrellas during the show!! (etc.)

But the odd thing is that this performance problem actually led to a national fashion trend, though I never got credit for it, thank God. But now it can be told — I was in fact and indeed the first comedian to push up his jacket sleeves.

I did it onstage, and then I did it before I got onstage. Next thing I knew, other comedians around me were doing it. And it looked better on them, dammit!!

Think I'm kidding?

Why would I lie about this? It was an inane thing to do, and even more inane to emulate such desperate behavior.

But officially, you must blame me.

I only did it so my forearms could breathe, honest.

Famous cartoon voices are always good for big, easy laughs. Too easy sometimes. By that I mean: If you can do the voices in the first place, there's nothing to repeating famous lines from famous cartoons.

But to me, as a comedian, that's lazy. You haven't written any new spin on them; you're just parroting. So I often tried to give a different perspective on these beloved animated icons. But starting with trademark lines was almost inevitable, for the recognition factor.

I did Tennessee Tuxedo characters, Mr. Magoo, Goofy, and several Jay Ward favorites. Especially popular was my Mr. Peabody opening recreation with comical choreography and kazoo accompaniment.

One character who never needed my material was Droopy. His dauntless persona defies parody, verbally at least. And the less he says, the better. Besides, Tex Avery gags are hard to improve — and, visually, impossible to do anyway!!

Customers and comics alike liked the way I was able to snap in and out of character in the ensemble pieces. So in one routine, I attempted to make the exchange between characters as fast as possible. The end of this popular bit (which I call "Deadly Duck") features a familiar gag written by Mike Maltese for Bugs Bunny and a certain lisping troublemaker . . .

Columbo: 'Scuse me . . . 'Scuse me, sir!! I hate to interrupt, but you are Mister Duck, aren't you?

Daffy: Begone, peasant. No autographs today, *if* you don't mind!! Hmf. Slovenly sort. Obviously a tourist.

Columbo: Uh, no, sir. The fact is I'm not a tourist. *(Showing badge.)* My name is Lieutenant Columbo — Homicide?

Daffy: Homicide? Homicide?! It's murder, he says!! Well, listen, flatfoot!! Ya can't pin nothin' on me, see?! 'Cause it just so happens that *this* little black duck is innocent. So -- *(Sticking tongue out.)* Mnyeahhh!!

Columbo: Sorry, Mister Duck, but I think you're guilty.

Daffy: Innocent.

COLUMBO: Guilty.

DAFFY: Innocent!!

COLUMBO: Guilty!!

DAFFY: Innocent!!

COLUMBO: Innocent!!

DAFFY: Guilty!!

COLUMBO: Innocent!!

DAFFY: *I* say I'm guilty!! I *insist* that I'm guilty!! And to prove it, here's two dozen glossies of me at the scene of the — *(Realizing his error.)* — crime . . . *(Huffing and puffing with rage.)* Columbo, you're despicable!!

Oh, uh — One more thing . . . ? I should mention I am a proud Columbophile. Years after I wrote this piece, I almost sold a serious script I prepared for this ineffably terrific TV character to Mr. Peter Falk himself, although unluckily for me, his contract stipulated the use of network-appointed writers only. Sigh.

Most often, to close my act at every club in and out of town, I would either detonate a Honeymooners bit, Deadly Duck, or — drum roll, please — *all* the "Looney Tunes" — all the ones I could master, anyway. [See APPENDIX I. for complete list.]

Occasionally I'd let a few 3-D characters lead into this: Telly Savalas as Elmer Fudd or Arnold again as (an Uzi-toting) Tweety.

But the response I'd get for the first Mel Blanc voice was usually thunderous. I'm not bragging. I wasn't even all that good at it back then. That was the overwhelming appeal of the LTs themselves!! I didn't have to write special material for them, as I explained. I did anyway, but it was really gilding the lily. If I didn't give the mob their favorite catch-phrases, then *they* would give 'em to *me!!* So I dug in on the homework big time.

And it paid off big time, because one day, I got a phone call . . .

I had been scouted (and taped!!) sometime in 1981 by an associate of veteran Warner Bros. cartoon director Friz Freleng, who was calling me out of the blue to critique my performance!!

Years later, when I privately met this animation icon, I didn't need to remind him of what he'd told me over the phone, "Your Daffy and Sylvester are solid, but work on the Bugs Bunny." And he recommended I start watching more cartoons to get the voices down because "Mel won't be around forever."

These were chilling words at the time, but he only said them out of concern for my possible future career as the Looney Tunes' vocal heir.

In the same paternal vein, he gave me some sound counsel on the subject of Hollywood phonies. "Some of them might not only try to wreck your career, but even pride themselves on being nasty about it," he warned. His advice was to ignore the jealousy and hatred of people like that, and stay on a positive track.

Mr. Freleng was very frank with me, very earnest, and very generous indeed.

To illustrate the point: it was Friz who gave Mel Blanc one of his own Oscars to fill the void that didn't allow this fabulous, fabled talent (and world-class Hambone Supreme) any major statuette. (And this was an Oscar that had been similarly given to Friz!!)

Of course, more about Mel to follow. But to finish up with Friz, I cherish the memories of my two conversations with him, another genius to be sure. And a sweet, funny old man who was more man than many I've ever met in Hollywood.

But I've jumped ahead a little too far, haven't I?

Let me close this chapter by earnestly intoning that Boston sure kept me busy. It was where I became a paid professional at last. And it was a hoot. As is appropriate for night owls.

Chapter 8:
So Then I Got a Day Job

As if I weren't busy enough, around the time I first heard from Friz, I was asked to function as the drive-time comedian by morning-show radio stalwarts Loren and Wally, then of WVBF-FM (They're now with WROR-FM) in Boston.

Loren Owens, a veritable Joke Machine, ex-Marine and very caring man, was already helming a morning-drive show with his on-air partner Wally Brine, a sports reporter and, with his natural gift for enjoying and spreading laughter, the perfect audience for comedy. They hired me right off the comedy stage to pop up every half-hour with a new minute of material, doing everyone from President Reagan to Rodney Dangerfield, plus several original characters to boot (e.g., my painfully unhip bandleader Sammy Stanza, whom I imagined as small and wearing a toupee. Listeners thought he was cute. So cute that, hilariously to me, no one ever asked him (or me), "Where's your band?"!!

I worked for "The Loren and Wally Show" about four years, and still have the cartoonish alarm clock Loren gave me to get to work on time!! (Not that I ever used it.)

Another extremely helpful friend from this era was the show's producer Tom Connolly, whose encouragements and spontaneous chortles I treasured daily. I hope these guys miss me only half as much as I miss them.

Daily radio was another learning experience of great value. Sometimes, because of the news or weather or who-knows-what, I had to write new minutes on the spot and squeeze them into the pre-news slots. I had to be *fast and* funny. And once in a great while they told me I was.

On the job, I must have exhausted my impression list at least twice, and my punning reached new heights of depths as I struggled to achieve and maintain my comic quality, if that's what you wanna call it.

Loren and Wally loved all kinds of comedy, so I inundated them and the listeners-out-there with not only impressions, but with regular original inanities based on sound alone, such as "People Who Sound Like Their Jobs":

JOE: *(Rapidly on-and-off mic.)* "Hi, Loren and WALLY!! Nice tO be here today!!"

LOREN: "And what do you do for a living, sir?"

JOE: "Me? I instaLL revolving Doors!!"

LOREN: "Get outta here!!"

SFX: (Brrroomp-CCHHH!!)

I still hear Loren's 8-track "rimshot" in my dreams.

And believe it or not, flighty folderol like this earned their rowdy, infectious laughter most of the time. (Loren was rowdy; Wally was infectious.)

On rare occasions, a caller would mention that they liked my work. More commonly, they'd try to top me or Loren, who was a pretty accomplished laugh-getter himself.

But it is a fact, of which we were all proud, that after we got going, we went from being the # 15 show to the # 2 spot in the Hub City's morning-show ratings race.

When I was asked to write to star in a TV ad to extol the addition of our new WVBF TraffiCopter, I prepared a slapsticky spot wherein I played a retro barnstormer pilot complete with goggles, cap and long, flowing scarf (sorta based on a character from Jerry Lewis's *The Family Jewels*). This went on to win a Clio award for the short-spot category. And it was very gratifying to see that award at the station every day, right by the front entrance . . . It was an excellent doorstop. (Brrroomp-CCHHH!!)

This FM radio gig also featured many visiting guest stars as well during these years.

Mickey Rooney was an incredible bundle of energy in his seventies. A tireless champion of countless charities, he was flown in by our TraffiCopter while we were on location for the Jimmy Fund at a golf course, and I'll never forget the sight of him *running* towards us, a good many yards, to get to the mic as Loren introduced him — What a pro!!

Henny Youngman was an hilarious in-studio guest, as much for his true personality as for being the original one-liner comedian. Coming in the front door, the first thing he did was to order breakfast. He then proceeded to unbuckle his belt and loosen his trousers as he sat at the mic. He asked for a newspaper and, reading nonstop, pretty much ignored us — until he was on. Then, as you might've guessed by now, the magic began: He unleashed joke after joke until we were all hysterical. Then when the mic went off, — "Where's that egg sandwich?" But the real capper is: After the show, he took *us* all out for breakfast!!

Another Joke Machine guest was the great and irrepressible Soupy Sales. I call him great not only because of his status as the best-known kiddie-show host of the '60s, but because of his fabled ability to deliver exactly what kind of laugh was needed at any given moment.

I call him irrepressible because his suit kept wrinkling. (Brrroomp-CCHHH!!) No, I call him irrepressible because I'd never seen such comic energy and professional focus in my life!! Arriving with no entourage and only a few written notes as guidelines, he spent a week with us, planning and directing comic bits by the dozen, in as warm and inclusive a way as any star I've ever worked with. I felt privileged to recreate his famous offstage stooges WhiteFang and BlackTooth. And he played straight for some of my skits too. He was an incredibly quick thinker and had an apt joke for everything, sometimes beating us to the next straight line as well. He was like a silly cyclone: Hurricane Soupy.

Carole King was a game musical guest. Easy to amuse, I guess, she told me privately how much she enjoyed my song parodies, which I'm still unfortunately writing today. (It is actually a curse . . .) (Okay, I'll name one: Ray Charles singing "Deck the Halls, Jack." Provide your own lyrics.)

Rich Little's straightforward professionalism and quiet humility off-mic was revelatory. I never thought of an impressionist as dignified, exactly, but I learned more than I even thought I would from him. And he was gracious enough to play "Ed Norton" to my "Ralph Kramden"!!

Canadian singer-songwriter Gordon Lightfoot ("The Wreck of the Edmund Fitzgerald" was also on the show. But I was extremely hungover that morning and can't remember a thing about him — a blur with a beard.

Wally did the sports, as I mentioned, and like most Bostonians, was very proud of the Celtics' near-mythical team of the '80s. We not only visited them at a practice once, but had them (and Coach Red Auerbach) in the studio more than once. The team's superstar was Larry Bird, you must remember. His natural wit, laconic delivery and willingness to kid himself provided a comedy godsend for me. During one day's visit, I offered our listeners a sitcom based on "The Andy Griffith Show," and set in his hometown of French Lick, Indiana. Every half-hour, Larry encountered characters patterned after Barney Fife, Floyd the Barber, Gomer and Goober Pyle, et al. Unquestionably, the station received more feedback on this nostalgic nonsense than any of my other work before and after. And the celebrated cager loved it too, laughing through every minute with Loren and Wally, to my great delight, though he blew his own punchlines doing that . . . Well, I can't hit a three-pointer either. (Brrroomp —) (See? I missed.)

Our most heart-warming visitor had to be Mr. Harold Russell, who in 1947 won two Oscars: Best Supporting Actor, and a special one for inspiring millions in *The Best Years of Our Lives*. A real-life World War II hero, he played Homer Parrish, the returning sailor who'd lost his hands, as Russell had. Knowing and loving this heartbreaking film, I wanted to give him some sympathy when, as we met, he offered one of his prosthetic hooks for me to shake, but I knew better. That was a character; this guy was beaming. Retired long since from the screen, he only rarely resumed acting (when requested), but was still very active in his "real job" as a charity fund-raiser, offering hope to those who need it. Meeting him was like meeting Lincoln.

Speaking of commercials, I worked for an incredible Show Biz legend, kinda-sorta, when WVBF personnel learned that Bob Hope was in town to do some charity PSAs for the Jimmy Fund. I was asked to write a radio spot for him — (Yikes!!) — thanks to that Clio. Then it would be sent to him, and he'd consider reading it if it suited his style.

Well, kiddies, I wrote it, and he liked it, and he recorded it, — but *not* as a radio spot . . . !!

I mean it was supposed to be, but Ol' Ski-Nose was recording for radio *and* TV that day, and somebody must've goofed because he recorded my spot for the wrong medium!!

So I'd just had the honor of having Bob Hope use something that I'd written, but something my radio station couldn't use!!

I'd have loved a dupe of that videotape, but Tom Connolly told me they just taped over it when they realized their mistake. Love that irony, baby!!

Yeah, and isn't it a pity Bob never got to meet me?

My best interaction, though, was probably with '30s Matinee Idol Lyle Talbot. Later a very visible character actor, his was one of those faces and voices you'd know immediately from any number of movies, radio and TV, usually playing a variety of authorities. Pretty much pushing Loren out of his own interview, I'm afraid I rather surprised the old gent with an encyclopedic barrage of his credits, from Charlie Chan and "The Adventures of Ozzie and Harriet" to big-bug sci-fi films and *Plan 9 from Outer Space*. I told him I preferred his Lex Luthor (in the serial *Atom Man Vs. Superman*) to Gene Hackman's, doggedly nudging career facts like these and more into our phone chat. Neither Lyle nor Loren were expecting such a well-researched, snap-memory tribute. (Wally thought it was funny; then again, Wally thinks *clouds* are funny.) And as it ended, you could hear the gratitude and gratification in Mr. Talbot's voice. For my part, it was a pleasure.

Once again, it pays to do your homework.

All right, I'm turning off the radio memories for one more chapter about stand-up, but don't touch that dial . . . !!

Chapter 9:
On – and Almost Off – the Road

By the mid-'80s, I was thinking about making the Big Move Out West. I'd already racked up hundreds of live shows, had tested my act on the road, booked around the country for about a five-year period ('80 to '85) through several different clubs, comedy agents and other comedians, in dozens of clubs, colleges, cafés and chicken coops. (Alliteration, like stand-up, is tough sometimes.)

By my reckoning, I visited forty states in sixty months, sometimes performing in two or more states simultaneously.

(Still paying attention . . . ? Okay. Just checking.)

It felt about that hectic sometimes.

Hey, let me tell you, though. Some of us love the road. Love the feel of adventure, the unique kick of seeking out and amusing new audiences every night. A new joke joint, new faces, new friends. The road for the road's sake . . . Me? I love "Magic Fingers" beds.

Then there was the time I thought we were all gonna die.

I wish I could remember who else was on this trip, but can't make a positive ID from the mug book in my mind.

Anyway . . . Imagine, if you will, that you are me, and that me is in the back seat of a tiny little car with three other not-so-tiny comedians, zooming down the highway back home from a typical gig in tiny little Rhode Island. It's a tiny little story I like to call . . . "A Carful o' Fear."

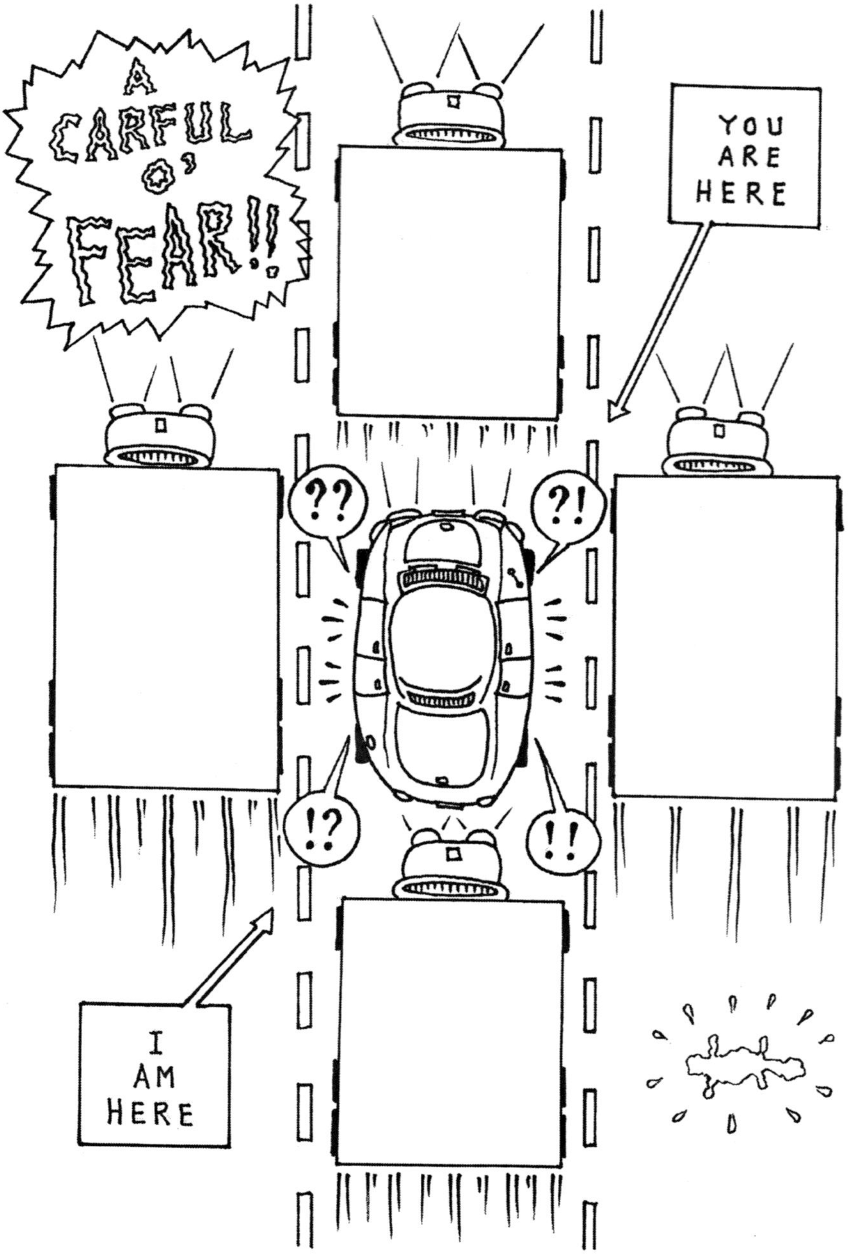
A CARFUL O' FEAR!!
YOU ARE HERE
??
?!
!?
!!
I AM HERE

It's the tiny little wee hours. Almost no one else is traveling the highway at this time of night. We're all tired, so any talk about the victories and vagaries of our various twenty-minute sets that evening is now over. All we wanna do is hit the sack.

Then . . . A Big White Unmarked Truck (BWUT for short) glides into view on our left, apparently ready to pass . . .

But instead, it locks in alongside us for a moment. Then it zigs around the front of us, — No zag, just the zig. — maintaining a steady speed. Okay, so he passed.

Seconds later, our driver says, "Huh!!"

"What," mutters my back seat neighbor.

"'Nother truck behind us."

Turning and looking, we see another BWUT, *right* behind us — textbook tailgating, as fast and steady as the one in front . . . *Precisely* as fast and steady, I notice. A tiny little frown now crimps my brow.

"The hell is *this?*" our driver scowls.

Just like that, his eentsy-weentsy little question is answered as another BWU, from absolutely nowhere, then a fourth identical transport, zoom into place on the right and left of us simultaneously!!

"Aw, Jeeze!!"

"Holy mama!!"

"Whut th' — ?!"

"What are they *doin'?!*"

We're not as sleepy now. Yes, we are riding, we four innocent laugh-makers, riding in . . . a Carful o' Fear!!

"We're boxed in!!"

"No sh*t!!"

"Why are they *doin'* this?!"

"It's a game!! Some kinda goddam road game!!"

That was it, all righty. For the next minute or two, which is long time if you're just staring at your watch, we were the meat in a great big, unhealthy BWUT sandwich. The driver was compelled to keep our speed exactly as fast as the four BWUTs were going, and that must've been close to 70 mph — doable, but in a spot like this, hair-raising!! More unprintable dialogue spewed forth like watery yellow mustard as we moaned, groaned, froze and prayed.

Then, as mysteriously as it began, it ended.

Shrieking as one, we lost control, careened into a fifty-foot construction pit and were splattered into detritus . . . And our ghosts still haunt Off-Ramp 19!!

No, I'm kidding about that part. But that is exactly what we all thought was *going* to happen!!

We later deduced that the playful pilots of these scary semis had obviously CeeBeed each other to give us boys a buzz for one of two reasons: (a) we were being punished for speeding (unlikely); (b) the sheer hell of it.

The correct answer is (b) the sheer hell of it. It must have been funny to them, but we weren't laughing.

And the moral of this story is: nothing. Some truck drivers are just sadists.

I wonder if the other three guys did *their* laundry the next day.

As if we were sports teams, a comedy rivalry between New York and Boston was already in place. (Apples and Beans don't mix, I guess.) Still, there was a fairly frequent exchanging of players.

Experiences we Bostonians had at some Manhattan clubs were frustrating in that we were made to feel unwelcome. Met with territorial scowls, muttered invective, playful challenges to step out into the alley, etc., it was like working with the Bowery Boys, directed by Scorsese.

I was put onstage too early and too late, and in one instance — too *soon*.

Here's what happened to me at the Comic Strip one night: Scheduled to follow a popular Manhattanite's killer set, I was standing by as the crowd cheered him offstage, about twenty feet from the steps. Before the applause died down, the indigenous emcee went to the mic and said only this, "Wasn't that great? Well, here's another of those Boston guys. Joe Alaskey," and walked away before the clapping had even ended, throwing the audience purposely off-balance.

It felt like the show had just ended. I hurried to the stage, which he'd left empty (more naughty host behavior). Audience members, given nothing to support me, started getting up and talking and ordering drinks. This guy just blew my opening to noisy smithereens!! — And it took me almost a whole twenty seconds to get 'em back, by gum!!

As I easily blew off his attempt to blow me off, I watched this guy, whom I'd never met before in my life, curl his lip at me. Yeesh!!

No sense mentioning his name. He never went anywhere.

And all because of what he did to me that night . . .

(A total lie, but now I feel better.)

NBC's "Saturday Night Live" influenced everybody and everything, of course. This unmissable TV show was then every bit as much the bulwark of the new age of comedy as George Carlin was its stand-up champion, tried and true.

A few years earlier, while I was still living there, shortly after its premiere, I was so desperate to try out for this show, I called their offices on the phone. I had no agent at the time, so what could I lose? All I wanted was info. So I call, and who do I get on the other end? Gilda Radner!!

I recognized her voice right away (I'm good at that). The show was only two weeks old, I think, so superstardom hadn't happened to any of them yet. Now let me tell you what a sweet, sweet gal she was to me.

First, she was tickled that I knew who she was, giggling and asking who put me up to this. After assuring her I was on the level, she actually started asking people there if they could help me, if there were more auditions coming up, etc.!!

For a second or two, I even thought I'd made a connection but she sounded disappointed for me that they were telling her to just hang up. But I'll never forget that ninety-second call. As for her, she had a fan for life, and that still goes.

Here's another story about NYC's "SNL" F.Y.I., okay?

At first, hearing that I was one of six or seven Boston talents invited to audition for Lorne Michaels (the longtime "SNL" producer) was quite impressive. If I knew how it would really play out, — !!

Well, looking back on it now, it's pretty funny, but at the time, we were all a bit upset.

Okay, so we all take the long ride and go to 30 Rock. We get there late afternoon. And we wait . . .

And wait and wait, standing and sitting and laying around. In a hallway. And then we wait some more . . . You guessed it. Local comics were asked in first.

In dealing with us, their invited, out-of-town guests, "SNL"'s "people" seemed not only unconcerned about the major delay they threw us, knowing we had another long drive ahead, but actually grew intolerant of our questions and understandable complaints.

Finally, we're called in to audition for the producer. It's now after midnight.

First guy goes in, comes out five minutes later, saying, "He's tired."

I'm thinking, "Well, naturally, he's tired. We're all tired. But I'll perk him up."

Next guy in and out: "Forget it."

Third guy: "He's wasted!!"

I was the fourth guy. 'Tired' was an understatement. Lorne Michaels looked like he was on death watch. His own. I did my stuff while the man's eyelids flagged, fluttered and drooped. His acolytes told me I'd done a good job, but I knew I might as well have been the Sandman.

This noddy debacle was an enormous waste of time by this time — for all of us. I just shook my wooly head and shuffled out, with a "Thanks, and pleasant dreams," hoping that sounded just mocking enough.

But here comes the punchline.

The fifth Boston comic was called in . . .

— and came out livid with rage!!

We were good buddies at the time, so I asked, "What the hell just happened?!"

"When I went in there, his head was in his hands like this —" and he showed me how that looked. "So I start, and a couple of seconds later, *he lays his head on the table and closes his eyes!!*"

"Yeah?!"

"Yeah!! So I went up to the table and *slammed my palms down on the table in front of his face!! That* woke him up!!" He then proceeded to tell the producer off in no uncertain terms. "How dare you" something-or-other about caring so little about "us Boston guys?" I forget the rest of the words, but you get the point. (This guy's still a comedy hero to me. I'd tell you his name but I prefer to spare the gentleman any potential embarrassment.)

I congratulated him for his honesty, and said it was too bad he had to blow off the audition in the name of justice.

But to Mr. Michaels' credit, this was not the case at all. He not only apologized, but agreed with my friend, stayed awake for him, and hopefully slept well afterward.

None of us made the final cut, though. (In fact, I don't recall any new faces but Bill Murray's popping up on "SNL" for awhile afterward.) But I learned in this instance that sometimes, even a producer can be a nice guy and a professional, even when sleep-deprived.

Our last tale of Manhattan (for now): If you're paying attention, you learn things.

I was doing a set somewhere — I think it was either
Catch a Rising Star or the Komedy Klone Klub, or the No-Boston-Comics Jernt. (Yes, I'm kidding.)

Anyway, one of my all-time favorites, David Brenner was the host and headliner. One of everybody's favorites, he had us all in his pocket, as usual. (People know when a performer loves them right back, and this man oozes love, la'ies 'n' gen'm'n...)

At the time, I was down on doing Gleason in every set. Afraid of being tagged as "that Gleason guy" (which I was henceforth anyway), I also wanted to see how well I'd do without him in my act from time to time. Comics who get associated with any specific routine often grow to resent it, and avoid repeating and enshrining it till they croak.

This meant that that night, I wasn't loving my job, and David rightly called me on it. I did fine, but when I came off, he returned to the mic, shielded his eyes and burbled, "Where's that big guy? Where's Joe . . . ?!"

"Here I am," I replied, pleased and confused.

"You know, *you ought to do Jackie Gleason!!*"

The crowd cheered, wowed by David's keen insight.

"Get back up here!!' Or words to that effect.

I sighed, though happily somehow. I knew what I had to do and did it. Out came the Bowling Routine: El Kill-o.

And Mr. Brenner's final analysis was, "You oughtta do that every time!! Right, folks?"

And with that, my fate was sealed, and I never copped out on doing my best ever again.

So thanks, David. You were right.

Another famous David gave me a tremendous boost in that city. But I'm trying to keep things in chronological order. So we now switch you back to our radio affiliate.

Chapter 10:
Is Moose and Squirrel!!

It was time for a turning point in my career, though I could never say I saw it coming.

In early '85, *The Loren and Wally Show* introduced me to two giants of the cartoon industry.

Naturally, Fate had to throw me a curve first. Off on a stand-up engagement over the weekend, I had just gotten off a plane and home around Sunday, midnight, ready to crash a few hours and revive for the morning drive, planning to go with pre-written material on file.

But first, luckily, I checked my messages (with an antiquated device called an "answering machine") and heard Loren say to be prepared with some appropriate material for none other than Rocky and Bullwinkle!!

It was the year of their marathon national 25th Anniversary Tour. Our live guests were to be Bill Scott and June Foray, the original voices for these still-adored characters. An electric shock went through my body!! So I turned off the answering machine and repaired those frayed wires (I told you it was old).

Throughout my childhood, I never missed that Jay Ward landmark show "Rocky and His Friends" if I could help it. Same went for "The Bullwinkle Show," "Fractured Flickers," "Hoppity Hooper" and "George of the Jungle"!! (And their many reruns.)

The show and our surprise guests were only hours away. Tired as I was, I was ecstatic!! Their visit had been quickly arranged but they'd been asked to do some stuff with me and readily agreed. So I kept my jet lag packed and stayed up all night writing three sketches dealing with their whirlwind tour in our Boston setting.

At daybreak, I went to the station, still physically exhausted but mentally charged. Coffee always helps.

My heroes soon strolled in and we met, cordially and officially. Loren had already told them about me and what to expect. My skits, along the lines of their classic comic cliff-hangers, featured furs-breadth escapes from Boris and Natasha's nefarious scheme to turn their tour into a fiasco, and incorporated the particularly windy weather Boston was experiencing that morning. I handed "moose and squirrel" their scripts. (Gulp!!)

Mr. Scott, who was by nature ingratiatingly avuncular, read them over quickly with a smile, then said to me, in a voice to which Mr. Peabody is most favorably comparable, "Yeah, we'll do these just as written." And the petite and charming Ms. Foray commented that no one else at any of the other radio and TV stations they'd visited so far had prepared such timely and/or funny stuff for them to do.

The ice was broken!! I felt great already!!

A few boisterous heartbeats later, I was reading with our guests' immortal animated counterparts live over the airwaves, and Loren and Wally provided the genuine laughs. Not that I wasn't pretty damn nervous about the whole thing, but somehow everything managed to click, and when the mics were off, both cartoon stars congratulated me both as a writer and as the voices of Boris Badenov (Paul Frees) and the Narrator (Bill Conrad).

After each "episode," the phone lines jammed (I think they would've anyway) with congratulatory and lemme-talk-to-'em calls. The skits were hits!!

To make a long, beautiful story short, Mr. Scott, who was also the modestly uncredited head writer and co-producer of all the famed Jay Ward cartoon shows, told me my voicework was the closest to the originals' he'd ever heard. Ms. Foray was equally, enthusiastically supportive.

I'm a doodler, by the way. My friends consider me the Emily Dickinson of cartoonists, as all my work is still unpublished (till now), and literally sitting in a closet.

Anyway, I started drawing Bill during one his phone-in Q-&-As. When we went to a break, he looked at my fine-line rendering and proclaimed, "*That's* not what I look like!!" And he grabbed a pencil and

a fairly accurate recreation of his spot self-portrait

—Bill Scott (drawed by hand)

"My Fractured Fairy Godparents"

JUNE FORAY

took about two seconds to squiggle a self-caricature, zany and hilarious and perfect.

"*This* is what I look like!!"

I made him sign it, instantly intending to frame and display it proudly at home, which I did.

And suddenly "Mr. Scott and Ms. Foray" became "Bill and June." I had very unexpectedly made two wonderful new friends who would figure significantly in my immediate future.

Because Bill backed up his words with a promise: If I ever wanted to move to Hollywood, he would help set me up in the animation business.

And, yes, he certainly did that. And much, much more.

But for me to open the door to this new opportunity unfortunately meant closing another. Yeah, the one with the doorstop . . . Loren and Wally, I can never, never thank you enough.

I miss our fun times together more than I care to admit. No joke.

Chapter 11:
My Best Shot

Loren and Wally understood when I explained to them that I might take Bill Scott up on his offer. While I made my plans, they would need to find and test a replacement for me.

I also had months of Boston-based and out-of-town club dates to meet. When I discussed my possible departure with my fellow comics and booking agents, I was urged to double my chances of West Coast success by entering the annual San Francisco Comedy Competition for 1985.

Not the most organized person in the world, I knew two attainable goals were better than one (or none), so I began to lay the groundwork to "Go West." I figured, "Why not?" Worked for Buster, Laurel and Hardy and the Marxes!!

And within nine months, I was on that flight.

It was right around this time that I got my heart broken. This is personal stuff now. Dunno why, but I've just never found the right gal. For a year or so, I was very good friends with a bright, lovely, kind young lady who was going to Boston College, majoring in education. I won't embarrass her by mentioning her name, but we broke it off when she was offered a terrific government job.

I didn't even try dating again for years. Then again, I've always been a "career guy." And often, the solace of the lonely is their work.

So now, I had a real need to succeed!!

The Golden Gate City and its Competition honchos treated me very well.

But even better, the first contact I had here was set up by Martin Olson, and his good friend (and everybody's good friend) Michael Pritchard met me at the airport — with cash!! (This was before ATMs were everywhere.) — and a place to stay if I needed it!! Michael was then and is now the patron saint of the SF comedy scene. His personal and professional charity work is widely known; he even ignored offers of stardom to dedicate himself to others. Even if I could thank him enough, he and his wife, writer Mary Jo, wouldn't want me to. Even Olson would make a face.

To give you an idea of what the point of this stand-up comics' contest was, it basically boiled down to exposure. The higher one was ranked, the more local write-ups and industry opportunities arose. They started with about thirty of forty contestants. Then we were winnowed down to the final week's field of five finalists — pretty standard stuff (especially lately, since it's caught on with TV).

Not standard at all was the quality of the comedians who entered that year. The participants included Rob "Defending the Caveman" Becker, Steven Wright, Roseanne (Barr), and Jon Stewart, all of whom finished better in Life than they did in this contest.

Two weeks hence, thousands of audience votes put myself and four other lucky guys in the top five.

In the meantime, I broke up a backstage fight between two anxious polar opposites, and who should have witnessed this courageous act but Roseanne, who when it was over, emerged from the wings to mutter to me, "You *stud,* you!!"

I mentioned audience votes, by which I was leading relatively comfortably as we entered the final stage, the winner to be decided in a live media event hosted by the witty A. Whitney Brown of "SNL" fame.

The way it was set up, though, on the last night, the decision was to be made by a panel of local judges whose names and faces were unknown to me and another out-of-towner who'd made the cut. Guest judges' assessments would be balanced with audience tallies from past nights. So I wasn't worried, pretty sure I'd continue doing well, though we all had to keep coming up with new stuff for every show.

In fact, going on last, I did better than ever, even with more obscure bits like Bud Abbott as a solo act (rapid-fire, bullying straight lines and insults directed cheerily at no one in particular). My four friendly rivals were also at the top of their game.

Now I have to be honest: earlier that night, I'd seen one of the local finalists socializing with some of the local judges being pointed out to me . . .

Came the announcements. In fifth place was — me.

I was pretty surprised. Thought I'd done better than that, frankly. But I got back onstage and hit my mark . . . to the sound of booing!! And people were shouting things!!

That's when Whitney Brown took the mic and explained to one and all that the boos they were hearing were "not for Joe." They were for the local judges!! And that what the people were yelling, in case you couldn't make it out, was, "Coke fix!!"

The rest of the announcements kinda fell flat after that, especially when the two local boys came in at Number One and Two.

To put it bluntly, controversy now ruled as the story hit the papers the next morning to add to the scandal generated by live TV and radio coverage and word-of-mouth.

The eye of the hurricane can not only be safe for anyone within, but at times even comforting. Everyone, from the Competition promoters to shock jocks scolded the judges and sympathized with me. This was better than winning.

(Actually, I hate telling this story, but these are the facts, Jack. And of course, I thanked the very principled Mr. Brown profusely for exposing the truth on the spot.)

Next thing I knew, the L. A. Improv was asking for me, and its owner, Budd Friedman, wanted to manage me (and did for awhile). The upshot was that I did better than win first prize. Within a month, I had won a career.

Simultaneously, I'd kept in touch with Bill Scott and could now fulfill my Funnymanifest Destiny. (No shame.) He started the wheels turning to get me into both unions (SAG and AFTRA) by putting me to work in an animated project scheduled to record just as soon as I could make my move permanent.

So it worked. I was on my way West. But not before all my buddies gave me a going-away party. They were stand-up guys, all right. They did impressions of my impressions, had a big cake and everything. I didn't want that night to end. (But I'm pretty sure it did eventually.)

This period was an unquestionably fun and productive time of my life. The whole experience felt like one big six-year bash -- even to the point where my friends and I had to "go home" when the party ended.

For me, it was just changing location.

Now things were happening fast!!

I found an apartment and went to work in La-La-land, playing packed houses and signing contracts with Budd, the unions, and my first v/o agent.

Anyone planning a move to any major city for Show Biz would be best served to fashion and concretize a similar plan, — then cross your fingers anyway.

Chapter 12:
"Hi. I'm Francis."

Francis is my middle name. But stop laughing, please. Because this story isn't about that.

What was happening to me was happening to dozens of other comics, comic actors, comedians, writers, and anyone who dared to step onstage and then made it work. For many reasons, including not-so-funny societal changes, stand-up had never been hotter. This you could tell just by going to the Improv on any given night — if you could get in. And join the shoulder-to-shoulder crowd. And everyone went, if only to get in the mix. Because the famous brick-walled showroom was at capacity almost all the time.

Waiting to get in, one sat at the open-space tables out front, shmoozed, networked, and made new friends.

I was waiting to go on one night and sat down face-to-face with a cool, bespectacled, shaggy-headed fella who was just kinda soaking up the buzz with a couple of gals. We smiled and nodded at each other.

"Hi. I'm Francis," says he. We shook hands.

"I'm Joe. I'm on in a few minutes."

"We're just here to eat tonight."

"Ah. Well, the food is great, isn't it?"

A nod, another smile.

Budd tapped me on the shoulder. I rose.

"Well, see you later."

"You're pretty smooth," murmured the canny owner/host.

"Thanks . . . Whattya mean?"

"What did he say to you?"

"Nothing, really."

"That's too bad . . . Know who that was?"

"Yeah. 'Francis'."

"Ford Coppola."

Duhhh?! My mouth was probably still hanging open as I took the stage. I couldn't wait to get back to table, just to say thanks for all his great work. But when I did, my seat had been filled. And I'm not the kinda guy who'd intrude on someone's dinner on my own behalf. Especially not with someone that cool. So I never did reconnect with him that night, a decided disappointment for me.

From that moment on, I resolved to develop my shmoozing skills to a more alert, inquisitive and attentive degree.

Lots of famous faces popped in. I met radio and TV vet Howard Duff (no relation to Hillary) and we shot the breeze about working in radio. He didn't think I was old enough to remember his "Adventures of Sam Spade." Kidding, I said I still used "Wildroot Cream Oil, Charlie" before confessing I was an OTR collector.

I watched forthright Mort Sahl tilt at the same old political windmills, Tom Dreesen excel at winning crowds, and fountain-o'-fun Robin Williams zap 'em silly.

Andy Kaufman's right arm and Comic Relief founder Bob Zmuda personally assured me, as he'd had to for years up to that point, that his late friend would not be resurrecting himself to blow the world's mind. And he shared some of the best Kaufman stories, some of which were written into the sincere and highly underrated biopic *Man on the Moon* over a decade later. (Jim Carrey *will* win some big award someday.)

It was there I first met actor/editor Chuck McCann, that adorable, humble and consummate man, though we ended up arguing over how to pronounce George Zucco's surname. Ya can't make this stuff up, folks. (We've been buddies ever since. And where's *that* autobiography?! Chuck's stories put mine to shame!!)

I remember telling a young comedian preparing for his first L. A. set to take deep breaths in order to settle his newcomer's nerves: one David Spade (no relation to Howard Duff).

And this was all on the same night!!

This joint was jumpin', all righty.

And was it there I first met Rosie O'Donnell? Or in Boston? Memory fades with age, ya know? You forget where you've been, what you've said . . .

At the San Diego Improv, I worked with other newbies like Brett Butler and Sinbad, and established talents like Emo Phillips, Sam Kinison, and, uh —

One's memories fade with age, ya know? You forget where you've been, what you've said . . .

Hold on. I'm almost through dropping names now.

Budd's Lake Tahoe room was where I met David Frye one night while opening (by personal request) for that "dull" teddy-bear of a guy, Jackie Vernon. After a brief conversation with Mr. Frye, he was mulling over doing a guest set for us — and did, though I missed him, darn it.

I had wandered over to a larger room to watch part of the G.L.O.W. show (Gorgeous Ladies of Wrestling), which was hot at the time. Boy, was it hot!! — In there. That room, I mean. (Whew.) Hey, it's all Show Biz, ya know?

Sorry, Mr. Frye, but I later ended up dating *two* of those swingin' sweeties that week. So it was more or less worth it, though it was a somewhat painful experience sometimes. You know how these things are.

And where's a referee when you need one?

On another occasion there, I was the middle act before the prolix, pungent Dennis Miller, and helped the opening act on her first road gig fine-tune some of her material. We even shared the same lakefront cabin for a week. Her name is Ellen DeGeneres.

(Oh, you're curious about that? Okay, I'll tell you what you're dying to know . . . It was the "Lassie" routine!!)

I've indulged myself so far in giving you, the reader, if that's what you call yourself now, a fully detailed self-portrait, including all significant experiences in different branches of Show Biz, to show you the path I took on my way to becoming a principle Voice of the Looney Tunes. (Okay, I coulda left out the lady wrestlers, granted.)

And I could write 88 chapters about all my on-camera experiences, but I'll try to focus more on my career as a voice actor. So I won't have to come up with a different title for this book.

Chapter 13:
Some Significant Signatures

At any rate, last time, you remember, the mighty moose and the plucky squirrel had invited their eager young East Coast discovery to move West and try his luck!!

After I'd found a place of my own, I called Bill Scott. This man, whose historic importance to animation was immeasurable, the co-producer, head writer and star voice of all that Jay Ward stuff, *insisted* on helping me make the actual, physical move to my first apartment in town. I still have the vision of him carrying my big cardboard boxes of Joe junk up a flight of stairs ahead of me.

To this day, I try to keep my ego in check as I recall the innate, automatic generosity of this — I'll say it and mean it — genius. As I've mentioned in many interviews, I started calling Bill my "Fractured Fairy Godfather" — and June Foray my "Fractured Fairy Godmother," of course. (If you're snickering at these nicknames, you may have lost the innocence of youth. Too bad.)

Bill was producing, casting and directing a new cartoon, an industrial sales tool for Union Oil he called *Return to Mocha*. I believe the plot involved training tips for executives in dealing with international trade. I was summoned to Buzzy's Recording in Hollywood, a favorite haunt for animavens (I gotta stop all this word-coining!!) who prefer a welcoming atmosphere with their technical expertise. I was lucky to have this place bestow my first pro sound studio experience. Even the engineers are laid-back friendly!! (Especially Andy . . . Hi, Andy!!)

I signed the SAG paperwork first, and waited for a handful of actors to finish some takes in the booth before meeting them. Again, the jaw dropped as, following Bill and June, out stepped Daws Butler and Janet Waldo!! These Hanna-Barbera stalwarts (Do I have to unreel their credits?!) seemed as pleased to meet me as vice versa. Also in the cast was that vocal wizard Frank Welker (whose credits are probably too numerous for his own autobio!!). "Privileged" hardly covers how I felt that day, on my first professional job in cartoons.

Almost forgot to tell you that I played, as v/o actors often do, several roles in this short. (— of which I never got a copy!!) (Stupid, Joe!!) (Well, I was new. I didn't know I could ask for one.) My favorite role was the stubborn, sarcastic island chieftain of the mythical Mocha.

To commemorate my induction into their ranks, everyone involved signed the cover of my script. Don't think I don't treasure that memorabilia!!

Bill kept me working as much as he could. I am very proud to tell you that one of those unforgettable engagements was in continuation of that anniversary tour. Many months after we'd met, I got to perform live with Bill and June at L. A.'s fabled (and now defunct) Variety Arts Center. Over the years, I played all their rooms, but my favorite gig was reading "Metal-Munching Moon Mice" — from Bill's original scripts!! — for a house packed with loudly enthusiastic fans!!

And — You like nostalgia? Get this!! — the opening act was Spike Jones (Jr.) and His City Slickers, complete with, among other original members, George Rock and Billy Barty!!

At the afternoon rehearsal, I was sitting near the back row of the audience, watching the band rehearse when the bubbly Billy, literally surrounded by little women (four at least), entered and sat near me. We were watching the band rehearse a non-Billy number when I heard him say he said he still had some chicken stuck in his teeth from lunch. I turned my head ever so slightly in his direction. He then asked one of the gals in his entourage for some floss. Then, floss in hand, he told her he really didn't know how to use it. I was tickled to pieces as he fumbled with the floss, unreeling too little, too much, and ultimately having her do it for him!! Only then did he look at me and shrug, so I could laugh out loud at last . . . He'd just done an impromptu bit for me and me alone!! Like Jolson and other born entertainers, an audience of one was enough for him, as long as that person was paying attention . . .

With apologies to (no relation, just their greatest fan) Keith Scott's wonderful book "Of Moose and Men," I have a correction to make. Keith was apparently never told that some voicetracks he attributes in that tome to his friend, the talented Corey Burton, who'd also done the Variety Arts Center show, were actually replaced by mine.

The voices were those of Boris Badenov and the Bill Conrad Narrator (same ones I did in Boston); the project was for the Bullwinkle Restaurant chain, in which Bill had an obvious vested interest.

I re-recorded hours of typically inane and hilarious scripts with him and June, replacing Corey's tracks. The new tapes (no CDs yet) were to be looped for customers' continuous enjoyment, and I still treasure my copies of these tapes. My guess is that Bill may not have had the heart to tell Corey (and thus Keith) that he'd decided to recast.

At any rate, it became a moot point as the chain folded soon afterward.

I called Keith and explained everything over the phone to him, offering not only this correction but a copy of Bill's self-portrait and a few interesting late-life stories as things he may want to include in any future edition of his book . . . Well, facts are facts, aren't they?

Most distressingly for me and everyone else who knew and/or worked with him, Bill himself passed on within the year I moved to town. His funeral service was filled with sadly smiling faces up front:

his family and those who knew him best, who understood that his quick passing was a blessing to him; -- and devastated younger folks and fans in back, weeping our fool hearts out that we didn't get to know him just a little better, just a little longer.

Then again, maybe Fractured Fairy Godfathers work a little better from on high . . .

As for that self-portrait of his, I look at it every day . . . (Wow. That was pretty corny, I gotta admit.)

Return to Mocha was my first job in a cartoon, and, for the record, my first on-camera movie role was as myself in a whoppingly bad turkey called *That's Adequate*.

But the movie wasn't!! My material basically boiled down to one tedious fat joke. I sure know how to pick 'em.

In the meantime, my late Uncle George valiantly drove his BWUT (O, irony, irony!!) with the rest of my belongings (which weren't much or many) down the narrow, winding street where I'd found my second place of residence.

Chapter 14:
Getting My Webbed Feet Wet

If you go back and check the Contents page, you'll see that the chapters get longer starting here. This is because your humble correspondent began to find himself in a constant whirl of Show Biz activity that's hardly slowed down for over twenty years.

I'm sure you realize it takes more than talent to do well in this business. You either need a good deal of good luck, or else it's "who you know" (or are related to, or sleeping with). And ten thousand or so hopefuls are still trying to find decent, or steady, or sporadic, or — How about *any?* — work at all, at any given time.

I just happened to luck out, true. But then I tried to make the best of whatever came my way, while remaining true to myself. They tell me I've risen to the top 1% of my craft. And not unscathed. But, as they say, I'm still here.

And I must thank two entertaining entities for the good fortune part of my durability: Jackie Gleason and Warner Brothers' Looney Tunes.

My first agent, Don Pitts, went way back. He handled many of the few actors who were sought out for regular v/o work in the "old days." We were delighted to be working together, and his number one guy was Paul Doherty (now a partner at another agency). These two introduced me to my first steady work and tons of other famous clients. Ready for more name-dropping? Good!!

Paul introduced me to one of his heroes, Bill Idelson. Bill started as a boy radio actor on the wry "Vic and Sade" and slid seamlessly behind the scenes to become one of the most diverse TV writers of the mid-century; he is the only comedy writer to ever have a script done on the classic "Twilight Zone" (his first script at that!!).

He in turn introduced me to my favorite living writer, Richard Matheson. (Anyone who doesn't know at least three of his volumes or production credits needs a better cultural education!!) Mr. Matheson was magnanimous enough to actually read a screenplay I'd written, and critiqued it favorably!! I've been writing ever since. (And there's the first of those more-about-them payoffs I promised you.) I have yet to follow his sage advice and try writing a novel, but I prefer the short story form and hope to see an anthology of mine in print someday soon.)

In Don's office, at Paul's desk, I also met and chatted with such well-spoken actors as Les Tremayne, Anthony Caruso and Jesse White. Jesse played a practical joke on me, offering hungry me some peanuts before reading some copy with him in the agency's booth. I hadda go floss and rinse first as he chuckled around his unlit cigar!!

Okay, let's talk about the Looney Tunes. (Only took me half the book!!)

In late 1985, the government asked Warner Bros. Animation to provide a PSA (public service announcement) asking folks to help save the "Wetlands." Daffy Duck was chosen to star, a most unlikely source of charity in any case. Mel Blanc was still with us, and I don't really know why he declined to participate, but it's no secret that his voice had weakened with age, and this was a singing assignment. The song was "Cheeseburger in Paradise" by Jimmy Buffett, and not being a Parrothead (fan of his) like my sensible nieces, I had to learn this song at home before recording it. The spot ran after prime time for years, making me both a Parrothead and famous duck simultaneously. And I was in Paradise, all righty, as I was told that I had just officially become Mel's first pinch-hitter in his illustrious fifty years as the Voice of Warner Bros.' Looney Tunes.

(Henceforth, let's call 'em "WB" and the "LTs," okay?

Incidentally, don't expect me to spell words the way LTs pronounce them (e.g., can you easily interpret the word *thethionth*?). "Type-lisping" only makes scripts much harder to write and read. Unless *I'm* typing, of course.)

By early '86, a handful of us voice actors were summoned to join what WB was calling their Voice Academy.

This entailed meetings with "suits," the dissemination of Mel's LT voice samples, and more homework: taped sound-alike assignments to be handed in for these executives' constructive criticism.

Our unofficial school was soon dissolved, however, as it became clear to one and all that direct competition through the process of standard auditioning was holding sway over this mostly noble attempt at teamwork.

What became the resultant Talent Pool (my phrase) boils down to four or five voice-actors who have enjoyed almost all the LT work to follow for two decades, including Bob Bergen, Maurice LaMarche, good ol' Frank Welker, and me. Others have come and gone over the years; a couple of them have stuck around, while others simply became unstuck.

I've heard comments to the effect that some of us were (and still are) better than others at reproducing certain aspects of Mel's voice placements, accents and impediments, his skillful acting and astounding versatility.

Whatever qualities exist in my work are the product of those many, many hours of self-ordered homework. That made the difference for me. To date, I'm the only one of us to have played all the best-known LTs for one project or another, and yeah, I'm proud of that fact.

And remaining a bachelor all my life has allowed me lots of spare time to enrich my vocal vocation and do my best. Oh, well. You heard the broken-engagement story already . . . "Lucky in cartoons, unlucky in love," I guess.

But the Academy never had a valedictorian; WB never officially picked a single successor to Mel Blanc.

For one thing, from the execs to independent producers and the ad agencies they hire, everyone's ear is different.

In addition, WB's own projects have consistently spread out the LT casting, which is still the case today.

Thus, the Talent Pool endures.

And WB has been most generous in the sheer number of jobs handed to me without auditions.

Then again, it's also true that we in the Pool were all continually auditioning for all voices, for the next ten or fifteen years, for almost every job. Tedious? Yep. But this was usually done to edify those independent folks who were overjoyed to be working with the LTs, and felt obliged to exercise their aforementioned ear. (Of course, power does not automatically bestow skill in many cases.)

I love my work. I felt then, and still feel, that my calling as a LT actor includes, as Stan Lee would say, a great responsibility.

The very survival of the LTs is at stake, and helping WB do that is most important to me. — Yes, more than the paycheck. And after this next, very pertinent backstory, I'll discuss the matter of casting in greater detail.

When *Who Framed Roger Rabbit* hopped into Hollywood in '87, director Bob Zemeckis set up auditions for two LT stalwarts that Mel would not be playing: Foghorn Leghorn and Yosemite Sam. After scoring both parts, I expressed immediate concerns about how Mel would take this news.

"Surely he'd been asked first!! — Is he angry? — How's his health?"

— etc. That's when I was told about his inability to deliver these louder, stronger-voiced LTs.

Not that he was unwilling to voice them, but he must have known that the characters he originated half-a-century before would now sound older and wheezier.

I still felt weird about taking over even one voice of his while he was still with us, and wrote him a letter saying I had mixed feelings about being cast in his stead, how much I appreciated being a new part of the LT legacy, but how I wished he could do them forever.

In return, he sent me a signed autograph: "Hi, Joe."

I didn't expect a letter, knowing how he felt. And when his autobio *That's not all Folks!* (co-written by Philip Bashe) went on sale, no mention whatsoever of *Who Framed Roger Rabbit*, in release by then, was made.

I thought, "Hmm. Well, that says it all, I guess."

I've been asked hundreds of questions over the many years. And questions like: "Why do the voices change from show to show?" deserve an answer in print.

But the answer is complicated, with human and business considerations that affected the gradual outcome.

So to satisfy the curiosity of so many WB cartoon fans, here's the story of the LT vocal legacy's evolution just as it happened, from my perspective as an insider . . .

I said "knowing how he felt" in reference to Mel a few paragraphs back; let me explain.

For years previous to *WFRR*, Mel showed up on daytime talk shows, and in addition to demonstrating how he did Bugs et al, he was accompanied fairly often by his son Noel, whom he jubilantly claimed would inherit his famous workload.

Now, it's important for me to say at this point that it is not my intention to trash Mel Blanc in any way. I can't fault Mel for pride in his accomplished son, yet Noel himself knew his father's dream would never materialize. By his own admission to me, he never had his father's voicebox, or even any proclivity towards acting. He's an excellent businessman, however, and a really nice guy. He just never had the heart to tell his Dad he didn't want to take over. Noel even gamely auditioned along with the rest of us for the Talent Pool after his father passed on, but dropped out rather quickly to pursue other interests, including marketing Mel's voicetracks in a number of clever ways (my favorite: the cuckoo clock).

As a result of all those talk show interviews with Mel, however, even today folks still tell me, "You can't be the guy!! I heard that Mel Junior (sic) took over for his Dad!!" There's your power of the media, and WB has never corrected this inaccuracy.

Towards the end of Mel's book, he insists that Noel's voicework sounds exactly like his, strongly implying the continuance of the LTs by birthright.

But virtually everyone disagreed with his evaluation of Noel's talents, including Noel. Like I said, *everybody's* ear is different — even Mel Blanc's. It was as if he simply couldn't hear (of anyone else occupying his post).

Although Mel's idealistic view of the LTs' future beyond his lifetime was confusing to me personally, all I could do about it was to do my best, and stay on a positive track, of course.

I hope explaining Mel's personal POV sheds light on the situation. But factually, his purposeful, paternal protectiveness put any possible transition from himself to the next-guy-who-could-do-the-voices on shaky ground.

I've talked about Mel constantly over the years but have never brought up this topic up before. And it's been hard to avoid. But on these pages, the whole truth is due.

So WB has still never officially specified, let alone advertised, any heir (or hare) to Mel's heritage. From the business angle alone, there are undoubtedly practical reasons why the notion of naming a successor to Mel has been rejected.

One major reason may be found in the moral of the following also-true story . . .

Under the powers-that-were when I first started, there was one other guy in the Talent Pool (whose name is *not* listed above). Though relatively inexperienced, he was given the chance to perform all the classic Mel Blanc voices whenever they were required.

Mel was still alive and mostly active when the Talent Pool was begun, and all of us in it understood that it would be most distasteful to try to undermine the man's hard-earned status by promoting ourselves as LT voices.

Almost all of us, that is . . . Because as soon as Mel died, this fella blatantly broke that unspoken rule.

He made a point of getting himself booked on more than one talk show, where he was proclaimed "the new Mel Blanc."

It must have seemed to WB as if he were attempting a coup, forcing them to acknowledge him. Apparently, he'd been asked twice by the suits to please *not* publicize himself that way. But he did it again, so WB kicked him outta the Pool for diving off the deep end. And he hasn't resurfaced at WB since.

The rest of us learned a valuable lesson from this, but a hard one: No More Self-Promotion, Ever. WB Animation would never again trust any of us to be the single voice of the Looney Tunes. That bridge was burnt by one actor, and now no one else would ever be allowed to cross.

Another reason may be purely financial. Business is like that, ya know. Mel got pretty expensive for his last twenty years on the job; after his thirty-year no-raise contract ended, his fee rose consistently. So might ours!!

But why promote a "new Mel Blanc" in the first place? That could be expensive too.

And the LTs sell themselves, don't they? My answer to that: Yes — as long as continuing quality is offered. Or else Golden Age LTs will become museum pieces, followed by works from the Digital Aged.

Yet another reason that was actually given to me once: "Kids would be disillusioned to learn that the LT voices come from human beings..." Yeah, right. And how's your old friend the Easter Bunny? This excuse is now and has always been one steamy cowpie. (Hey, I do have fearless opinions after all!!)

So there's the story, as I understand it and lived it.

But despite everything, roughly twenty years since Mel's passing, it's clear that the lovable Looney Tunes stars will undoubtedly outlive everybody. — Me too, I hope!! I'd hate to think I killed them!! — and continue to shine with the help of many generations of creative cartoon-makers to come.

Back to *WFRR*: I went to work as Foggy and Sam sometime in '87. Unusual in that he recorded my tracks on an indoor film set, Mr. Zemeckis was happy with my interps.

Also unusual was their major scene together: a funeral sequence!! I don't think it ever made it to the animation stage because, I was told, it was deemed to be too dark for the rest of the film. The funeral was actually a bogus ceremony, whereby Roger's pretending to have expired so he can avoid more trouble as he and his friends proceed to solve the mystery. Foggy had a four-page speech (!!) eulogizing Roger, while Sam carried the coffin, grumbling. Other characters with dialogue cut from the film included Casper the Friendly Ghost, Popeye and Olive Oyl.

I met and worked with sweet little-old-lady voice vet Mae Questel on the set. We both still had dialogue by the final cut: Sam goes sailing over a wall as Eddie Valiant (Bob Hoskins) first arrives at the studio, and, though Olive got the axe, Mae voiced Betty Boop, her original claim to fame, in the nightclub sequence, also featuring that fantastic Daffy-versus-Donald piano-dueling duet.

Mr. Hoskins was at the premiere, and he was a riot that night. He had me in stitches mock-complaining about the rigors and uncertainties of interacting with "nothin' but thin air for two years!!" He articulated enormous relief that the shooting had finally ended, but that he still felt dizzy.

"Cel-shocked?" I grinned. He liked that one.

WFRR won four Academy prizes, including Best Editing, Visual Effects, and Sound Effects Editing. Animation captain Richard Williams received a special Oscar for his breathtaking efforts (though perhaps his cameo as Droopy really cinched it for him).

For its impact on the industry alone, it might've even gotten the Best Picture nod, had it been nominated. And the screenplay, adapted from Gary Wolf's novel by Jeffrey Price and Peter Seaman, was also worthy of winning!! And what about Bob?! Not even nominated!! (But Zemeckis would win for another movie in which I appeared. Like I'm some kinda good luck charm? Good luck with that theory!!)

Happy ending: *Who Framed Roger Rabbit* was a roaring success, won many, many other awards, and became the vanguard of an animation boom that lasted quite a while.

Unexpected anecdote time!!

Right around the time *Roger* was released, I chanced to be working one day at a sound studio called Waves, when Noel approached me. Mel was just finishing up, and Noel asked me if I'd like to meet him (finally).

Well, of course I did!! After all, there was much more to love than not about this historic animation pioneer, maybe the best the business will ever hear.

A few minutes later, Mel, using a walker, emerged smiling from the booth, and continued smiling as his son introduced us to each other. I pretty much reiterated what I'd said in my letter, and, still smiling, he thanked me for helping him on the movie, telling me I "did a fine job." Then, about thirty seconds later, he shuffled off into eternity literally for me, smiling, smiling . . .

This was our one and only meeting.

WB was ready for the aniboom and felt strongly they'd strike gold with "Steven Spielberg presents Tiny Toon Adventures." It was a fail-safe concept: the LTs have adolescent counterparts, ya see, and they sorta kinda act just like their heroes and instructors at Acme University.

My agents Don and Paul said to pick whichever character(s) appealed to me most from the breakdowns' descriptions. I thought it best to go with just one character, the one patterned after Daffy. His name, of course, was "Mucky Duck." According to the show's creators, he should sound like a born loser, as egotistical as his animated antecedent, and "have a lisp like Daffy's, only different." I interpreted this as meaning that this character would carry most of the potential comedy, as Daffy was always the biggest laugh-getter of all LTs.

That quote about the lisp didn't confuse me at all, by the way. I had long ago mastered several types, and knew Daffy's was essentially frontal. I opted instantly for the lateral lisp, formed on the back teeth (Thank you, Morey Amsterdam of "The Dick Van Dyke Show"), pitched Daffy's voice an octave higher and then just thought like Mel. This they liked, and I got the part, thanks in part, I'm sure, to first-rate voice director Andrea Romano.

It was quite a workout!! Unhappily for me, I was in a great deal of pain at this time of my life, suffering with that redoubtable hip and lumbar disorder, sciatica. It took a major weight-loss campaign, years of therapeutic exercises, and acupuncture (the combination of which finally did the trick) to beat this monster back. I dealt with this "Ag-o-nee, ag-o-nee!!" as best I could, so I guess I'm a trouper.

But once, when my character's cue was a scream of pain, it came out so loud and horrible that the engineer had to whip his cans off!! I later apologized profusely to him and Andrea when I further realized I hadn't given him time to adjust my volume level!! Yeowch!!

By the time we recorded the first show, my character, Mucky, had become "Plucky Duck".

Who changed the name? Um, that'd be me . . . !! Andrea told me the writers weren't sold on his original moniker and asked me if I had any suggestions. Luckily, I'd given this some thought already, and, last-minute as it was, the name was changed officially very near the hour we were slated to sing the show's theme song!!

There sure was a lot of singing on TTA, I gotta say!! Scared me at first!! I'd had some experience in musical theatre, but never took a lesson in my life, unable to read music due to almost-total left-brain malfunctions that to this day have kept me from going beyond grade school math!!

Yep, I'm dyslexic in a weird way. All my life, I've been reading backwards and forwards and anagramatically, instantaneously; but numbers and simple directions have always confounded me. For this reason, I've never been able to drive a car either (I also have a fear of going over 30 mph). Wanna laugh? Ask me to point North, South, East or West sometime!! I can't do it!!

But I *can* deliver a punchline. And there was some good comedy writing on this show, make no mistake. The program's entire concept was called too derivative by purists, but they didn't object as robustly after the premiere.

This show also had chipper chatterboxes Charlie Adler and Tress MacNeill as Buster and Babs Bunny (no relation to any other bunnies); Danny Cooksey as Montana Max (a new age Yosemite Sam, Ah plumb reckon); Cree Summer, hilarious as pet-torturer Elmyra; Frank Welker as an updated Wackyland Dodo; and many, many more too numerous for this paragraph.

My favorite episodes, in no particular order, include:

- "PLUCKY'S DASTARDLY DEED" (Betraying best friend Hamton resulted in his first confrontation with conscience.)

- "SLUGFEST" (A scathing satire of Teenage Mutant Ninja Turtles —like that was hard!!)

- "TTA MUSIC TELEVISION" (No v/o by me, but savvy shtick set to the eccentric tracks of They Might Be Giants.)

- "HOW I SPENT MY VACATION" (So good they released it in VHS & now DVD — also my nieces' favorite!!)

- "DUCKLAHOMA!" (which audibly stretched my poor voice an octave higher, and the episode that saw the birth of anvil-mania.)

- "THE HORN BLOWS AT LUNCHTIME" (I also played Yosemite Sam and, for a change, Porky Pig.), and —

- "THE RETURN OF BATDUCK" (for fan reasons alone).

But my absolute favorite is the very last one we did:

- "NIGHT GHOULERY"!!

Plucky was prominently featured in well-researched and finely-tuned (-tooned?) pastiches of three classic horror stories, "The Tell-Tale Vacuum" which pitted his diseased mind against Hamton's cleaning mania, complete with baroque, Poe-like dialogue; "The Devil and Daniel

Webfoot" (which allowed me to play the other lead this time); and the best of the three, "Hold That Duck." This one features Buster Bunny and Plucky as Abbott and Costello respectively (and respectfully), based on their 1948 hit *Abbott and Costello Meet Frankenstein* (which was the first movie I ever saw in a theater, in re-release). I knew the material inside-out by the time this gem of a script fell into my hands, and producer Tom Ruegger, who voice-directed me this one time only, let me have my head as I meticulously reconstructed Lou Costello's side-splitting verbal antics, adding variations where needed. This hour of horrific hilarity is also still available while supplies last.

Contrary to popular opinion, I did not play Baby Plucky; that was done by Nathan Ruegger, the producer's son, who was approximately that character's age. In other words, I'm not that good an actor!! I did voice Plucky's patient Dad, however, using Mel's real voice. (But all *you* ever remember is "Wada go down da hoooole!!")

We had guest stars too. One unforgettable day, Broadway superstar Carol Channing came in, asking our permission to work without her wig. (No, she's not bald, silly . . .) Coincidentally, years later, she's become very, very nice to my niece Trish, who designed her website.

That uniquely gifted comic actress Edie McClurg, with whom I worked on game shows, played Hamton's Mom (Mrs. Pig) in "Vacation," as drolly as ever.

Cast as Mr. Wade Pig was a true Show Biz genius and survivor, the superlative Jonathan Winters. My first encounter with him was glorious, glorious . . .

I arrived at the "Vacation" taping session during the lunch break. About nine or ten actors and techies were all standing in a semi-circle in the parking lot, all facing Jonathan, who, unmistakable from any angle, was in the middle of telling a story.

I got out of the car, his back to me, and approached the group.

Without stopping his improvisation, Jonathan reached out, took me by the arm as I passed him and began making me a character in his nutty narrative!!

Ham that I am, what else could I do but get into it? — although just being in his fabulous presence was a tad daunting!! For years, I'd wanted to meet this guy, and now, in so doing, I've become some obtuse gas station attendant he's trying to dicker down by pretending to know all about motors!! Keeping my face as straight as possible, it only ended when we were called back in to work about three minutes later. Then he suddenly wondered who I really was, and he said he really liked the way I worked. "Ya got right into it, didn'tcha? Good for you!!"

In the booth a minute later, he blew a line, then blessed me with a tremendous laugh when I told him: "Your motor's stopped running." Getting to work with this world-class, one-of-a-kind comic was better than getting his autograph, which I'd always wanted too, but under the circumstances, totally forgot to ask for!! To wrap up my story, I not only did Plucky, but subbed Jonathan's singing "99 Bottles of Beer" and several porcine yells, and lived in seventh heaven for about a month!!

Later, I inherited the Wade Pig character by default for two more TTA episodes, in case that matters to you. It did to me!!

When Steven Spielberg visited our booth, he signed autographs for all present and added to mine, "Whenever I talk to you, I need my shirt dry-cleaned!" — Well, he was in a hurry. (But little did we know how our paths would cross again in the near future . . . !! Yep, another teaser.)

I found out after the fact that Vincent Price had provided a voice for us in one episode. (No, not J. Evil Scientist; that's an urban legend.) I wasn't in it — can't even recall the title!! I had yet to meet Mr. Price (Teasers "R" Us!!), but I did "cover" his voice, as we say, again providing a blood-curdling shout beyond, alas, another esteemed actor's by-then enfeebled capabilities.

Now let me say a few words about Don Messick, who played Plucky's neat and clean pig sidekick. (I just hadda love any character named Hamton!!)

I'd never experienced working with a quieter, more dignified soul than Don, who resembled an owlet more than a piglet, frankly. (Fans of "The Duck Factory" sitcom with Jim Carrey and Teresa Ganzel know this already.) We worked pretty tightly together as Hamton and Plucky on TTA. Don made me laugh so much as a little kid, along with Daws Butler, on all those early Hanna-Barbera shows, I couldn't help but love — no, *revere* the guy. And what a pro. I think he had only two fluffs (bad takes) in three years with us!!

I have one funny story about him: At his busiest, Don was known to commute for hours every day between L. A. and home. Then he and his wife moved to Santa Barbara.

Hearing this, I asked him if that wasn't even further away than his last residence.

He said, "Yeah . . ."

"Well, doesn't that mean you spend more time driving?"

"Yeah . . ."

"And less time at home with your wife?"

And he replied, twinkle firmly in eye, "Yeahhhhh . . . !!"

He knew a good straight line when he heard one!!

"Tiny Toons" enjoyed a spate of product associations: toys, dolls, its own breakfast cereal, fruit snacks, plasticware, snow tires, wrecking balls, Fabergé eggs, you name it. (Hey, I'm only human!!) (Most of the time.)

The Monday-through-Friday show's popularity was further proven when we were all invited to participate in a radio project designed to encourage kids to read, "Mrs. Bush's Story Time." (This was Barbara Bush, not Laura.)

She read children's stories to us toons (I also did Daffy and Sylvester for this series), all of whom who were written down a few years to reflect our target audience.

The upshot of this project's predictable success led to an official invitation to the White House to meet the First Lady herself. (She didn't record her lines with us in Hollywood.)

So, one crisp Autumn day, we all met Mrs. Bush in the Rose Room for the media and a few laughs. She was sociable and ingratiating in person. But what an idiot *I* was!! I'd forgotten to pack a suit the night before we flew in and had to go meet the President's wife in a sweater!! (But a dignified one; no moth holes.) As we shook hands for the cameras, I just had to apologize.

"Look, I'm sorry about the sweater. Guess you can tell I'm a voice actor." I got a little good-natured razzing for that gaffe by my colleagues, but I also got my laugh.

A rather unexpected perk from TTA was "The Plucky Duck Show," a worthy spinoff that spun itself out quickly due to stiff Saturday morning competition. Ooo, those #$%<?&@!! "Teenage Mutant Ninja Turtles"!! But, man, what a temporary thrill!!

At this point, a lot was happening in my stand-up career. And I'd begun an on-camera career as well.

So maybe I'd better backtrack for a quick recap of some of those events before the I relate the next phase of my life as the cat, the canary and the duck.

Chapter 15:
Busy, Busy, Busy

*T*hen there was the time I kidnapped a UFO . . . !!
   Well, no, I didn't. I just said that because a chapter this boring needs a little goosing up. Maybe I should go back to those G.L.O.W. girls and —

Oh, you're not bored? Even better!!

Anyway, as a by-product of the animation boom, the traditional LTs and old favorites from other studios enjoyed a brief renaissance period themselves.

From Miracle Whip and Target to MCI and Sprint, from McDonald's with Charles Barkley and old radio pal Larry Bird to Gatorade with Michael Jordan — and back again, Bugs, Daffy, Sylvester, Tweety, Road Runner, Wile E. Coyote and company were active in the commercial world. Video games, followed by CD albums, followed by Welch's jelly glasses, followed by DVDs, spewed forth.

I was especially self-impressed when I sang Yosemite Sam's personalized version of "Help!" in only two takes!! (The CD is "Bugs and Friends Sing the Beatles.")

WB and Steven Spielberg further presented TV series like the highly-regarded "Animaniacs" (no relation to the TTA episode of the same name) and "Pinky and the Brain," and less successfully, "Freakazoid!" and "Toonsylvania." And while "Taz-mania" triumphed and "Histeria!" tanked, new films leaped into the planning stages.

Concurrently, Jay Ward's Rocky and Bullwinkle franchise returned for a Taco Bell campaign. I was Boris to June's Natasha again, dollink; and I even got to re-voice my mentor's last starring role, George of the Jungle, for his return to TV for a season, if only in promos.

My voice was also heard on an NBC special which imported Britain's "Spitting Image" puppet-caricature show. In "The 1987 Movie Awards," I helped shishkebab several American movie stars: Woody Allen, Paul Newman, Dustin Hoffman, William Hurt, Burt Lancaster, Robert Mitchum, Walter Matthau and Leonard Nimoy's Spock as the villain.

Before Jackie Gleason died in '87, he'd hired me to loop some time-eroded dialogue for Ralph Kramden previous to the release of "The Honeymooners: The Lost Episodes."

The reason he needed a replacement was because by then, years of hard drinking and constant smoking had pulled his own voice into the deep gravel.

I was told he randomly picked my taped audition out of a field of two hundred the first two out three times.

And the episode where lovable moax Ralph had the most to say (again) is called "Lawsuit," which, of course, I recorded wearing my old diaper. Seriously, I still can't believe this show is on my resumé.

Having this incredible credit, I was also invited to do some v/o as Kramden for CBS's salute "Jackie Gleason - The Great One." Through this two-hour special, I met John Candy (who was kinda depressed in general that night, poor guy), Jane Kean, Audrey Meadows and Art Carney. The ladies were spectacular. Mr. Carney, whom I held in awe, seemed every bit the gentleman and professional I'd heard he was as we shot some of his on-camera antics as Ed Norton hearing his buddy's voice (me) from the beyond!!

Sweet and supportive Suzanne Somers was doing a TV special and had a "Honeymooners" sketch with a modern twist: Alice Kramden becomes liberated in color dream sequence when Ralph gets knocked out accidentally in black-&-white. She chose me to play Norton — No, just kidding — Ralph. Norton was Maurice LaMarche. And the skit worked well, although they forgot to make the "old" footage monochromatic!!

Not too long after that, I was flown to NYC to do a commercial for Braun shavers which used footage from "that timeless "Chef of the Future" Kramden-Norton classic with new tracks provided by me — and Art Carney.

The atmosphere was wholly different now, and he and his wife asked all about me and requested a few bits from my Bad Casting act. Making a giant of comedy laugh made me tremble with warm disbelief. And he told me some great inside stories about working with Gleason. Wish I could repeat them here. Nothing new, really, but I don't think Mr. Carney would want me to.

Then writer James Bacon tried to get a miniseries about his friend's life, based on his book, made as a CBS miniseries. To make a long, painful story short, it didn't happen. His widow Marilyn's wishes to stop the project were honored because she actually controlled the rights to Mr. Bacon's book (?!). In fact, her phone call to CBS was made the day — the very hour!! — I was there, set to sign the contract!! A great opportunity lost, and yes, I was there, literally present when Mrs. G's call came. It woulda been the shining jewel of my career up to that point, and if I'd let it, it woulda eaten me alive!! But, hey. Life is too short. And, — Oh, well. You can't eat a Fabergé egg.

Even later, towering talent Brad Garrett did the bio as a TV movie, and though I found the script surprisingly gloomy, with not enough of Gleason's material recreated (to suit me, at least), I had to give Brad three solid stars.

And lo!! A very heavy monkey had been lifted from my back!! I had long since wearied of being identified as "that Gleason guy," remember?

So, thank you, Brad . . . Now do Aunt Sadie!!

Lastly, I finally did get to play the rotund laugh-maker (gotta get a new thesaurus) in the 1999 TV movie *Muhammad Ali: King Of The World*. For the historic Clay-vs.-Liston fight, The Great One had bet against The Greatest, and despite my suffering a horrible flu that week, I had a ball doing a scene with the capable and friendly Chi McBride at ringside and wading waist-high through the warm-water Miami Fountainbleau pool bar set . . . Anybody see it?

Whoops!! Better take my time machine back to the shop for repairs while we scoot back to 1986, because this is one of my favorite stories.

Even more embarrassing than my brush with Mrs. Bush, I think, was my meeting William Shatner, another Don Pitts client. I went up to the office to audition one day and Paul asked me if I'd like to meet Captain Kirk.

"Well, sure!!" I beamed. (Sorry.)

"He's got a great sense of humor, and I'm sure he'd like to see your impression of him."

"Hmm!! Really?" I was intrigued and a little scared. Not of him, per se, but of doing anybody famous for that person directly one-on-one. Summoning my last ounce of courage, I agreed to do this.

But he was in the booth, and Paul added that he was here on a quick break from the set of *Star Trek IV: The Voyage Home* and had to go rushing back.

Many agencies have a door to facilitate fast celebrity exits, and when Mr. Shatner was done reading, he bolted for this door. Here's the thing: He was in his vivid Admiral's uniform, orange makeup and all, and almost out the door when Paul called out, "Wait a minute, Bill!!"

He turned, his hand still on the doorknob.

"There's someone here I want you to meet."

As all my favorite Shatner performances zipped through my mind at warp speed, I smiled nervously and approached him down the short hallway, my hand extended.

He raised his other hand in instant stop-signal mode.

I froze (and just about dematerialized.)

"I'm — *sorry!!*" he warned in his most halting delivery. "but I . . . *never* — shake hands with — strangers."

Homina-homina-homina . . . (as Kramden would say.)

What would *you* think?! I didn't know what the hell to do now!! My hand was still outstretched, and as I started to slowly withdraw it with a face that I'll bet resembled an unloved, half-squashed tribble, he blurted:

"I'm kidding, for Chrissakes!! Put 'er there!!"

Paul howled as I re-inflated myself and said, "You got me!! You really got me!!" And I was thinking, "Oh, thank God!! He has a sense of humor!!"

I should've known better, and sooner, but then again, he is a terrific actor!!

"He does the best impression of you," finished Paul. "You've gotta see it. It'll only take a minute."

"Go ahead," the pumpkin-hued Admiral nodded.

So I did the Annie Hall "but we need the eggs" joke, which did amuse him, I'm pleased to report. But he got the last laugh too when he concluded, "Very good, very good. But where were you when I was reading for this stupid beer commercial?!" And back he went to his starship and crew.

And today, of course, he's still one of the best actors working today, and one of the funniest. And now everybody knows it!!

One of the first jobs I landed was the television series "Out of This World," which started as part of NBC's five-sitcom bloc to change primetime to 7:30 PM. Ours was the one that lasted, though we were syndicated the second year. It starred Donna Pescow as "Donna," Doug McClure as a dopey mayor, and Maureen Flannigan as Evie Garland, the preternatural pre-teen sweetie who talked to her absent alien dad via candy box. (I still don't get it.) Scripts varied from silly to — Well, mostly, it was just silly. But fun. Some of the writers went onto "The Simpsons," where the writing suddenly got much better!! (Maybe having 19 extra "producers" per show helped.) And Steve Burton, who played Evie's boyfriend, graduated to Emmy-winning work on "General Hospital," where he's been ever since!!

One of the most distressing events at Universal Studios, where we taped the first season, was the infamous fire that destroyed the historic *Frankenstein* exterior set. And our sound stage was directly involved in the story. Whoever set this fire (and arson was strongly suspected) had sent the studio's firefighters to us while the conflagration blazed some distance away, fast and furious. (Luckily, there were no casualties. Just outrage and disgust at the loss of some key cinematic history.)

I worked with another cast member, John Roarke, an excellent impressionist famous for his George Bush, Sr. and stint on "Fridays" (of Andy Kaufman "fistfight" infamy).

This was a political puppet show, "D. C. Follies." My mainstays were Jimmy Carter, Andy Rooney, John Madden and a really goofy Gerald Ford. Funny lady Louise DuArt was the first season's third, distaff member of the voice cast. Together we let the politicos really have it, and appeared as guests on ABC's "Good Morning, America" and "Nightline." Dependable Maurice LaMarche replaced me for the second and final season.

I enjoyed the passel of interesting guest stars on both these shows during their simultaneous run. During "Follies," I made a minor connection with Steve Allen, who cared about a lot of people because he was just that nice a man; and vivacious Betty White, who later asked

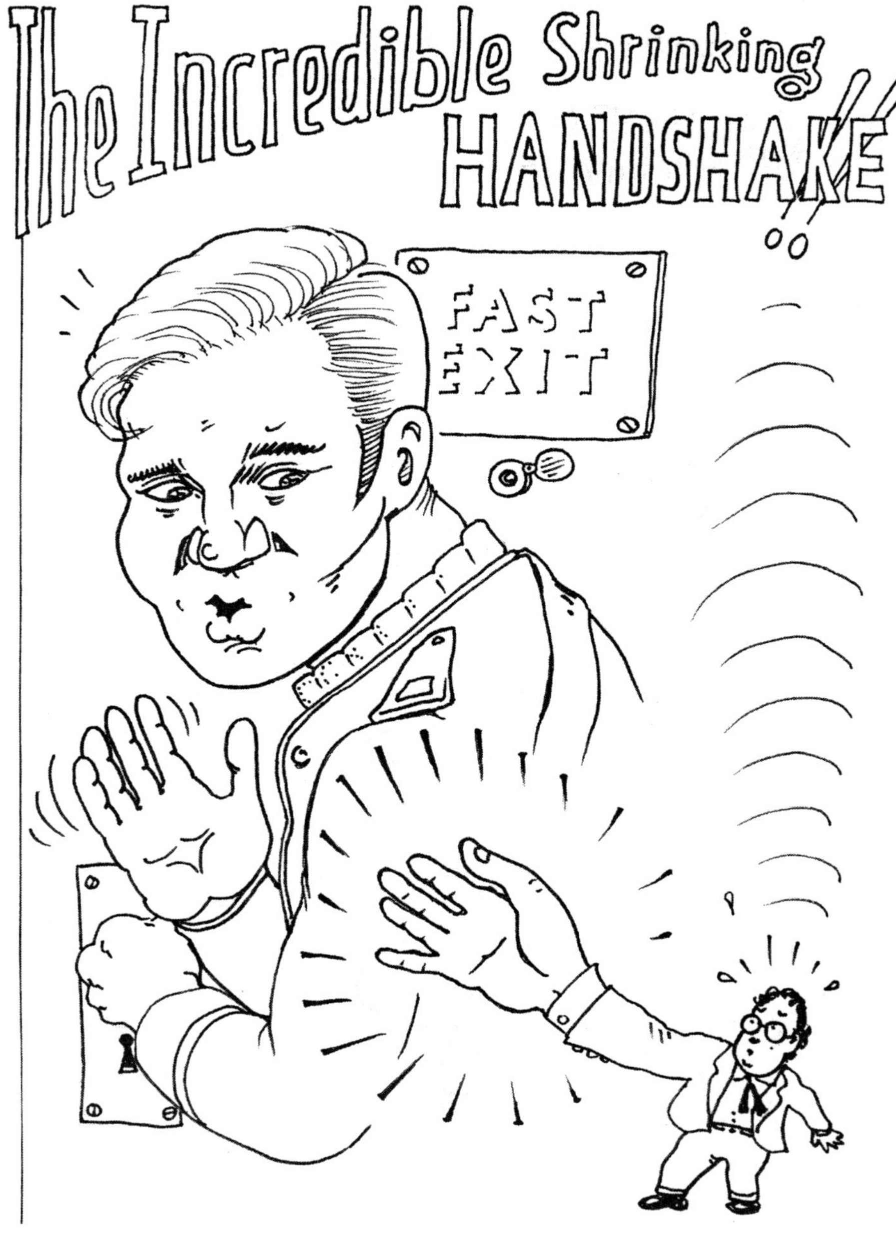
The Incredible Shrinking HANDSHAKE!!
FAST EXIT

for me to do a bit on "Golden Palace." (Both these entertainment greats signed autographs for my Mom.)

On "OOTW," some of our visiting luminaries shared some great Show Biz stories: Ann Miller, Ruth Buzzi, Richard Kiel, Jamie Farr, Betsy Palmer, Herb Edelman and Frances Bergen (Edgar's wife and Candice's Mom).

But my favorite had to be Larry Storch, whose perfect concentration and comic timing ranks with the best. When we weren't trading Edward Everett Horton impressions, he regaled me with many uproarious, unprintable tales of the legendary Lord Buckley. (Much more about His Lordship and Prince Larry later.)

Doug McClure and I became good friends almost immediately. What a wonderful man he was to everyone. Unflaggingly positive, naturally funny, humble and big-hearted, he was a professional inspiration and the biggest kid on the set. We all loved him for himself. Our star, Donna, who'd made a similar bond with him, and all of us on the "OOTW" were devastated when he died suddenly. But at least he didn't suffer, never knowing what hit him (Cancer works fast sometimes). But I know I still miss the man.

One of the unforgettable things Doug did for me was to get me an invitation to the 1990 Golden Boot Awards, which is really a banquet and elaborate excuse for people who work(ed) in Westerns. A lifelong fan of the genre, I was dazzled (hornswoggled?) all night long, and the year I went, that room was overloaded with the biggest-name cowboy stars, character actors, directors, stunt-folk, etc.

Imagine getting to meet and talk with Roy Rogers and Dale Evans, Clayton Moore (the Lone Ranger, kiddies), Katharine Ross, Cesar Romero and Iron Eyes Cody -- all in one night!! The "masked man" even gave me a private demonstration of some fancy holster-work!! (Thought I was gonna faint till he gave me that famous grin!!)

Oh, and Doug and I sat with Burt and Loni, they of the famous link-up. (Burt was the voice of Evie's dad, by the way, but this was our first meeting. And Loni was a doll.)

Also present were Marie Windsor, John Ford stalwart Hank Worden (ninety-plus, he drove himself there!!) —

— and one of my favorite all-purpose players, soft-spoken scene-stealer Dabbs Greer, whose most high-profile exposure was probably as Reverend Alden on "Little House on the Prairie." I sat with him and wife for a good quarter-hour, unraveling so many of his credits he almost cried.

"And I thought I was still an unknown," he murmured.

"You made his night," Mrs. Greer told me.

"My *night?* You made my whole *year!!*" he said with a delivery I know you can hear.

And talk about a survivor? Mr. Greer went on to do *The Green Mile* (as an aged Tom Hanks), and "Lizzie McGuire"!!

Though I'm not usually an autograph collector, I made sure to bring a book that night!!

My last Western note: Years later, I got Gene Autry's last autograph, so I was told by his secretary.

Anybody wanna sell me a "Gabby" Hayes?

1986 through 1995 were extremely active years for ol' Joe (or "Snow" if you prefer — my family nickname).

As an actor, I did "Head of the Class" as a stuffy poet; "Growing Pains," as the Devil in a dream-wedding sequence that got cut, darn it; and "Night Court."

On this one, entitled "Author, Author," I etched the poignant portrait of a Peeping Tom plumber hauled before the judge, Harry Anderson, by a pre-"Nanny" Fran Drescher, for whom I predicted great things, right to her face. (Wonder if she remembered how right I was?)

That's show's ingratiating character star Richard Moll took me to lunch that week with a buddy of his, an up-and-comer named Tom Hanks (These cycles are endless!!), who'd just wrapped *Nothing in Common* with Jackie You-Know-Who. No, I didn't inundate him with questions about his co-star . . . or about his own career either. (Sometimes "lunch" is just that: lunch. Sorry. No refunds.)

Richard later returned the favor (kinda), when he guested on "OOTW" as Evie's driving instructor.

Director Barry Levinson auditioned me for, and cast me in *Good Morning, Vietnam* . . . !! Yeah, wow. But contractual obligations to "OOTW" prevented me from taking the role and flying to the shoot in Bangkok. Robert Wuhl got it instead.

What's that? Pity? Forget it!! As TV's Uncle Beano, I got to switch personalities with a cute li'l puppy dog and give everyone beehive hair-dos . . . !! Job security, baby!!

Another cool audition I had and lost was for *Postcards from the Edge* (the part ultimately played by Rob Reiner). At least I made Mike Nichols laugh.

Earlier, I auditioned for Rob Reiner himself, for a summer replacement sitcom, though his notes seemed far more interesting to him than I did. (I later learned the part had already been cast.)

And another loser was my tryout for a Russian-based TV comedy special for the brilliant Billy Crystal. This guy walked in and said: "Hi, Joe" before anyone even told him my name!! Impressed *me!!* And what a pleasant soul. Maybe he knew me from stand-up.

I was pretty hot, I gotta admit, doing varying sets on many live-audience showcases: that "Comic Strip Live" with John Byner in Hawaii, "Comedy On The Road" (again with Byner), Budd's "Evening at the Improv" (more than once), the fledgling Comedy Central (throughout many network name-changes, in clips), and the famous "EtCetera Show"!!

(No, wait. That's a typo.)

Merv Griffin invited me to do four of his shows from Hollywood, though I got "bumped" once by former TV phenom Bishop Fulton J. Sheen. No, I didn't complain, — for God's sake.

And in May of '86, I was asked to do a six-minute spot on Late Night with David Letterman, with less than a day's notice. It all went down so fast I hardly remember the details, but they had to fill in for an ailing monologist. So I was flown into town ASAP. Next thing I knew I was backstage at 30 Rock.

I got to pick my entrance music, and bandleader Paul Shaffer liked my choice, "Yakkety Yak."

Watching the show from the green room suddenly turned nightmarish. A then-popular series star was purposely antagonizing David by taking a picture of him (knowing he doesn't like that). David cut the interview short and went to the commercial, tangibly upset.

This should've made me nervous, but in the wings, I thought, "Well, the way that segment just went, I'm either gonna go over big or fall flat on my face."

Dunno how I did it, but I killed — standing "O." I did Woody Allen and William Shatner as each other, the Nicholson/Haskell and Romeo & Juliet bits, and of course, Kramden and Norton.

Cheered up, David called me over to his desk for a little chat. So the host liked the guest — Yay!! I answered a few questions and did Don Knotts as Abraham Lincoln. He suggested I don't look like some of the people I impersonated. "And someday I hope to direct," I added, getting a laugh out of him. He also plugged my New York Improv gig twice, and I was there at the sign-off.

Minutes later, he and Paul stopped by the dressing room to thank me for saving the show. Then I got an informal studio tour (which houses things like a closetful of industrial pipes vividly painted by Muppeteers).

I wondered if I'd be asked to return.

Gee, I hope it's soon . . . I'd love to pop up on one of his currently-popular Impressionists' Weeks. I bet I'd hold the record for between-show breathers!!

My career took an unexpected turn when the game shows started asking for me. I did quite a few of them in a short space of time, the worst part being that they have to separate the celebrities from the contestants. So I missed a great big bunch of dating opportunities with some of those honeys!! Oh, well. They were just there for the cash anyway. (You're not taking all of this seriously, I hope.)

The truth is that it was all fun and games!!

I think my first one was "Win, Lose or Draw." Burt Reynolds (again?!) co-produced with Bert Convy, and they were on the lookout for celebs who could use a squeaky black marker as fast as their wits. I was on the second week (with mirthful Marilyn Michaels, delightful Julie McWhirter Dees and steady Fred Travalena. Hmm. Guess it was *their* Impressionists' Week.)

I got to know Mr. Convy better when active actress Nancy Stafford and I did "Super Password" and found him to be a super man. No red cape, exactly, but that week, he was named "Father of the Year"!! And I won a happy contestant $15,000. *My* paycheck got lost in the mail, though. (JOKE!!)

Then I was a Hollywood Square — twice!! I swear . . . !!

And on that show, I met Milton Berle, for corn's sake!! (And this time I really mean "corn," brother!!)

There's a story that goes with this: Uncle Miltie had a long-running ratings rivalry with another comedian who has not remained nameless, but now I'm tired of typing his name out over and over.

Anyway, before the taping, one could hear a loud family-style argument coming down the corridor from the Berle dressing room.

Shadoe Stevens stuck to the shadows. Even Rip Taylor looked intimidated, confetti curdling in his pocket.

We remaining eight Squares all held our breaths, but the big issue had been resolved by the time we were called to the set. Mr. Television was still a tad tight-jawed as he passed by me at the door, but he was ready to roll.

We did two or three half-hours, wherein I did my thing as his infamous, well-upholstered rival, wondering what his reaction would be (if any). (Wish I'd had a monitor on him at that point!!) Then we all took lunch.

I began to exit the studio when I felt a hand on my arm . . . Yes. Milton Berle had grabbed my arm!! — an action for which he'd been a bit infamous himself. This gesture was something he was accused of doing when preparing to upstage a bigger laugh-getter. Racing through my mind just then was the Show Biz story of how Gleason (There, I said it.), guessing he'd do this to him one night, had lined his jacket sleeve with a platoon of straight pins!! The result, "Yeowch!!"!! And here I was, "that Gleason guy," getting my arm grabbed by Milton Berle!! Yeesh!!

Well, he didn't recoil in pain this time. He did position himself in front of me, though, and looked me dead in the eye, the luster of his wet-paint-slick scalp just close enough to smell. Then he pursed his lips, nodded, winked, — and patted my arm. And walked away.

Somebody said, "You know what that was? Know what that meant? He liked you!!"

And I said, "More than that. He *approved* me."

For all his past frustration with Gleason, even after a blow-out in the dressing room, and despite having had to be in a room with Jm J. Bullock for over two hours, he was benevolent enough to do that for me. And if you don't think that his appreciation and approval, though wordless, from a man who'd lived as a star since his childhood in Vodvil, is unimportant to the recipient, you don't know beans about real comedy. (And sorry for the wisecrack, Jm, but you really shoulda stayed in your own square while I was on!!)

On the contemporaneous "Match Game," I was proud to be working again with Betty White, and others too numerous to research... Oh, okay. Ross Shafer was also host to snappy celebs Teresa Ganzel (that living doll), Sally Struthers, Bill Kirkenbauer, Ilene Graff, Daphne Maxwell Reid, Jonathan Prince, Deborah Harmon, Vicki Lawrence, plus Chris Lemmon and of course, the heart and soul of that show, Mr. Charles Nelson Reilly. I give him a formal title because he deserves it. He put us all at ease, exhibiting natural warmth and generosity. He gave me five bizarre neckties.

Chris Lemmon was right at home too. The first guy I met before the shooting, he pulled me into his dressing room like an old friend to watch the Three Stooges (and me practice a Jack Lemmon/Walter Matthau bit for the cameras), and talk comedy.

Doing game shows was great, and again I managed to win a five-figure prize for a player on one of those Big-Wheel-double spins, by matching "*Blank* Rabbit" with "Roger." What did they think I'd say? "Bugs"?! (That contestant bumped into me only a year ago, gratefully recounting every detail of that lucrative week for him. I think I would've too!!)

A celebrity "Family Feud" week offered me a double reunion when I was asked to team with Norman Fell and good ol' Soupy Sales, sharp as ever. Also on the team was former "Tonight Show" writer Pat McCormick, whose wacky way with words made him famous enough to develop his own act, cut an album and become a comic actor, teamed with waggish songwriter Paul Williams, his physical opposite. Adding quirky-jerky Charlie Callas, we became the "Funny Men"!!

To no one's amazement, we battled the "Funny Women" and, as in real life, came out about even. The youngster of my group, I never had a such a "Funny Week" in my life!!

The only damper on these proceedings was the startling subsequent suicide of host Ray Combs, whom I'd known from the stand-up scene, and who obviously never developed the tough skin our business requires. Career setbacks and personal tragedies are bound to happen. But even when, at times, it seemed I'd lost everything at once and that everyone was against me, as he did, I never felt that utterly hopeless, and hope I never do.

Unsurprisingly, I got a game show of my own, one "Couch Potatoes." The game was fairly standard: three-person teams vied for standard prizes answering host Marc Summers' standard TV trivia questions, interrupted by the announcer (me) who was "actually" the "funny neighbor" next door who watched the show's taping (somehow), from, naturally, his sofa... I think I've got that right.

But wait!! There's more!!

For eighty shows, this announcer/neighbor, who was also a spontaneous impressionist, volunteered automatic TV parodies complete with costumes and makeup, even though he lived alone. Now I'm confused, aren't you? I believe this premise was created by Mr. Potato Head, now my sworn enemy.

In fact, my participation afforded me free rein to write, direct and portray random characters and scenes from classic programs. Old buddies Olson and Rafferty helped me with the scripts, providing two-thirds of my material.

And in case you're interested, the best spoofs were probably: a hungover Captain Kangaroo fed up with his puppet pals, Julia Child fed up with a revolting recipe, and well-fed upstart King Tut from "Batman" (heroic ham Victor Buono). Other favorite bits: "Kojak" reading poetry, a "Superman" crook with kryptonite in a lead box, explorer "Marlin Gherkins (Perkins)" opting for the couch instead, Jonathan Harris (cowardly Dr. Smith of "Lost in Space"), a multi-character "Twilight Zone" tribute, an overexuberant Jimmy Stewart in *It's a Wonderful Life*, "The Millionaire" spritzing his envoy with seltzer, Howard Cosell calling TV ratings like a horserace, "Howdy Doody" liberated from his strings (I beat Martin Short to this one), Freddy Kruger played by Jimmy Durante, Nixon's "Checkers" speech (delivered while shaving), Robert Vaughn selling hair restorer, Andy Devine being cruelly manipulated by "Froggy," my secret admirer Roseanne, PeeWee Herman as a crashing bore, Fred Flintstone looking for a new series, David Janssen's "Fugitive" in need of a headache remedy and a better prosthetic arm, Marlon Brando's *Godfather* wielding a potato peeler at the Five Families meeting (Sorry, Francis.), "Zorro" as a bad magician, and many lifts from my act. And, not missing a trick, some of these original pieces were also adapted *to* my act.

I know that paragraph was a lot to digest, but it was my show, ya know? I only wish it had lasted longer; I had a mad, hectic ball with this format!!

And, even better to me, the show was spiced by the inevitable surprise guest stars from the medium's past and present. I'm not ashamed to say the presence of some of these old-timers was oodles more exciting for me than even doing my own bits, and we had dozens of 'em!!

Among them were ol' smoothies Steve Allen and Soupy Sales (couldn't get away from the guys!!); Donna Douglas, the erstwhile Clampett clansbabe; and Chekov from "Star Trek," Walter Koenig. I single them out because they were so approachable and generous with their time.

But none more so than two real heroes from my youth, Noel Neill and Jack Larson!! Whatever good karma brought this about, I couldn't wait to talk to them!! And it was downright idyllic to discover the "secret identities" behind their familiar guises of Lois Lane and Jimmy Olson.

I expected them to be amiable and accommodating. What I didn't expect was *their* awareness of *me!!* When I thanked Ms. Neill for all those hours of baby-sitting, she rejoined that I was providing the same service for her whenever she baby-sat her grand-kids, as "Out of This World" was their favorite show!! (No kidding. She knew details!!) And Jack loved my John Hamilton (Perry White) impression!! I'll leave it to you to imagine his reaction when I bellowed "Don't call me 'chief'!!" at him!!

To top it all off, they took even more time with me to openly share memories of George Reeves, the array of beloved character actors who graced the "Superman" sound stages, and their current lives — stuff even my many research books couldn't provide!! Bless 'em both, that's a day I'll always treasure.

I did a game show pilot with the elegant, long-reigning First Lady of Entertainment, Jayne Meadows, whose acting always shone as bright as her beauty. She was aware I'd worked with her husband Steve a couple of times already and, ever the lady, gave poor pedestrian me a ride home, quite out of her way, in her chauffered Rolls Royce.

Seated next to her, I felt like royalty myself.

"What was it like working with Steve and all those puppets?" she asked me. And "Did he like the script?" And "Did you say you'd worked with him on another game show?"

Questions like this made it unmistakably evident how deeply she loved her man. It was genuinely touching, and I think I fell in love with her myself just then. Who wouldn't? Who couldn't?

Jay Leno had me on a few "Tonight Show" sketches. As a regular player for a while, I did Ralph Kramden twice, as a Hare Krishna, as Bill Clinton's bus driver (made sense at the time), and, last and least, *The Godfather* trying to scare Barbara Bush by putting orange peels in his cheeks (?!), which bombed audibly. Hey, I didn't write 'em, folks.

In retrospect, if I *had* actually kidnapped a UFO during this period of my life, I probably woulda forgotten it a week later.

Chapter 16:
You Can Do Anything in a Cartoon!!
(Almost.)

*M*ost of that is a line from an old Tex Avery cartoon. I only add the parenthetical disclaimer because while on the job I found out otherwise!!

Specifically, I found out that no cartoon character (not even one with super-powers) can sniff a flower till it's pulverized, and then inhale it.

Sound familiar? This was the controversy that marked the otherwise welcome "Mighty Mouse: The New Adventures" during its second season back in '88. And I was there.

Our producer, tough-as-nails Ralph Bakshi already bore the stigma of notoriety, but I think he kinda dug that, since he picked it up for giving the world its first X-rated animated feature, based on Robert Crumb's underground comic book, *Fritz the Cat*.

But his "Mighty Mouse" was drastically overhauled and sitcommy, essentially a semi-nostalgic twist on the old 20th Century-Fox fare which also reflected the current times.

The modern angle is what got him in trouble, of course. Mighty's powder-snorting seemed to energize him unhealthily in the eyes of media watchdogs who saw this action as a thinly-disguised cocaine reference. I couldn't tell ya what Ralph and his co-writers really had in mind, if anything. I wasn't in that episode. (And if that sounds like a cop-out, then just count me among the undecideds.)

I can tell you I had a blast lampooning the likes of Kirk Douglas, Cary Grant and Edward R. Murrow, as well as one classic TerryToon character, Sourpuss (a Jimmy Durante type). (I'd have preferred to do Oil Can Harry.)

And my first day on the job, there were gasps in the recording booth when I said what I said . . . to the boss.

Let me explain. Ralph has a tremendous, abrasive New Yawk sense of humor. And he uses it to push the envelope with actors sometimes, to get the best out of them.

But I knew dis goin' in, see? I'd been warned he was gonna needle me. Yeahr, aha . . . !!

So there I was, trying my best to please him, but he only seemed more and more frustrated with me, until he barked after my third or fourth take, "Man, that sucked!!" — getting the requisite shock laugh.

All eyes turned to me for the reaction.

Heh heh heh. I had my punchline already, see? So I revvs up me timin', den I sez —

"Ohh . . . That sucked?" I deadpanned.

"Yeah, it sucked!!"

"Well, you oughtta know," I acquiesced. (Gasp!!) "You're the expert on 'suck'."

Jaws plummeted. Eyeballs bounced. Klaxons blared. But Ralph fell out of his chair laughing. Then we all laughed. The cast and crew loved seeing him get topped even more than me sucking. So, bulls-eye. We had a great relationship after that, with no more temper-tests or prefab sarcasm.

Too bad he's not as active these days. Ralph's a good man, which is more than I can say about some producers.

In the late '80s, strip cartoonist Berke Breathed oversaw a special based on one his Christmassy Opus story, "A Wish for Wings That Work." I provided voices for five characters: Truffles the Pig, three

Stooge-like ducks and two-thirds of all the dialogue for a cross-dressing cockroach originally voiced by Dustin Hoffman!! (In cartoons, you see, Ham definitely trumps Method.)

Continuing to voice films, I did a Dr. Strangelove sound-alike in *Spaced Invaders* (Sorry, Peter Sellers fans, but that's exactly what they wanted.), good ol' impressionist-lovin' David Letterman himself in *Wilder Napalm*, and the title role (sorta) in the TV movie bio *Kingfish* (really starring John Goodman; I voiced the "Amos 'n' Andy" radio star whose name Huey Long borrowed).

Skimming along in my time machine, we find me in a key v/o role in Bob Zemeckis's *Forrest Gump* (1994), starring Tom Hanks. Bob said he hired me as President Richard Nixon because it was the most realistic replication he'd heard. I won't give away the film's excellent gag here, but it always gets a major reaction from viewers. And wouldn't ya know I've got a good story about this experience too?

Bob called me to his Paramount set on the last day of shooting. Almost nobody was around; I thought I'd gone to the wrong location. Then Bob bopped out to greet me and tell me this shouldn't take too long. However long it took was okay with me. I wondered if Tom would remember me from that lunch with Richard Moll 8 years ago. Probably not.

"By the way, Tom's a little punchy today. He hasn't had much sleep."

Okay, definitely not.

But "This should be interesting," I mused.

It got even more interesting than that.

When all was ready, a loose-limbed Tom arrived on the green-screen set, also explaining as we met (again) how he felt a mite exhausted. (And again,) no problem.

With me sitting in a front row of audience before a makeshift proscenium, we rehearse the brief scene once or twice (as I shift dramatically to present tense) . . .

Quiet on the set . . .

Then I hear Bob's voice, "Joe, how tall are you?"

Question marks surrounded me.

"Six feet? Er, six-one?"

"Perfect."

Yeah? For *what?!*

"Get up onstage with Tom. You're the same height as Nixon." Words to that effect. Guess I was a little punchy too. "See that blue mark? Stand there."

Now Tom and I are facing each other. He's weaving now, and smiling like a mischievous kid.

"Hey, Tom, do you remember we had lunch about eight years ago with — ?"

"Hey, I'm just trying to remember my lines, Joe!!"

Fair enough. I smiled.

"Okay now, you're standing in for Nixon now. You *are* Nixon," directed Bob.

Then Tom started joshing me about this, amused I was called to double-duty.

"Yeah, you're Nixon now!! C'mon, get into it!!" I forget the actual words, but Tom was challenging me in a chummy schoolyard style that proved his punchiness and started to crack me up.

Well, old habits die hard, so, taking up the gauntlet, I just snapped right into the face, the stance, the whole Nixon thing. But realistic.

Now Tom starts to giggle.

"You gonna do that?! This is my last day on this!!"

"Do what?" the President inquired.

Tom enjoyed my lean, premium hamming and only getting into character himself kept the fine, younger-than-me actor from losing it for a second or three. Then *he* started trying to crack *me* up, but I was a very well-rested pro. Eventually, I had to stop doing the impersonation so we could get through it more easily.

I hoped I hadn't burned a bridge to Bob, but it worked for his star. Tom latched back onto his now-famous Gump creation and we did finish up quickly at that.

No real punchline here. But love it or hate it, and I think audiences overwhelmingly choose the former, this movie went on to win six Academy Awards, including a tandem, post-*Philadelphia* prize for punchy ol' Tom.

I think it's a great film, and I don't throw that word around, you'll notice. (Wait. I just did a word-search. I throw it around like confetti... Well, anyway, it's a stupendous, voluminous, multitudinous film. (Yeah, I got that new thesaurus, thanks.)

Two other, quite strange v/o ventures worth mentioning were for *Glengarry Glen Ross* ('92) and *Blade* ('94).

For the first, I was hired to clean up all that naughty, Pulitzer Prize-winning language for the "airplane version." I'd never said, "Forget you, pal!!" before in my life, let alone 19 times in a row. I laundered a total of seventy-five lines — and that was only for Jack Lemmon!! (Wonder why he didn't wanna do it himself?)

When we met at a mall years later, Mr. Lemmon treated me with polite reserve when I mentioned that job, but sparked when I mentioned working with his son Chris. He also marveled at my Bugs Bunny, and by request, I gave him his best buddy Walter Matthau, though he was called away before we could get into lines from *The Odd Couple*!!

For *Blade*, I provided all the dialogue for Pearl, an enormous, repulsive vampire; and for the President (or whatever) of the parasite planet. *This* guy required me to lip-synch everything he said, never an easy job, — *in his native (fake) language.* (Funny, he didn't look Gibberish.)

At the same mall, I later met the hypnotically gifted Shari Lewis; her show had spurred me to do hours of hand-puppet shows for my little brother (when we *were* little).

By this time, I'd finally found my ideal agent. In no time, he helped make me one of the workingest v/o actors in town, the "Top One-PerCent-ers."

Thank you, Vox, Inc., and thank you, Wes Stevens.

To my great surprise and glee, I got the chance to work with June Foray on a series, and we were overjoyed to be working together again — but this time every week!!

This was WB Network's "Sylvester & Tweety Mysteries." June was already "in the bag" as her definitive Golden Age Granny while Andrea Romano conducted auditions, as usual, for the title LTs. Evidently, the voice choices for these two proved to be difficult. I was told that when some sort of casting stalemate had occurred, WB Animation staffers were played nameless sample tracks of all finalists, and I ended up with both parts. As with "The Honeymooners Lost Episodes," I won by democratic vote!!

I always wanted to do a whodunit series and "S&TM" is the closest I ever came. (I'd rather play the surprise killer than the detective, actually.)

Plots generally had Granny and her squabbling pets (including Hector the bulldog — Frank Welker) visit different countries and cultures around the world, solving various crimes. No murders, naturally, but poor, ever-screaming Sylvester was the weekly victim of severe comedy-writing abuse!! Tweety usually perpetrated most of the puddy-tat's punishment (So what's new?) while helping his sleuthing mistress find the answers. All seniors should have a hobby, don'tcha think?

I can't really decide on a favorite episode, we did so many beautifully designed and imaginative stories. As ever, some were better than others, and the quality was such that we enjoyed a robust five-year run.

And that wouldn't have been possible without creative minds like Tom Minton, Karl Toerge, James T. Walker & Charles Visser behind the scenes.

There were always plenty of "usual suspects" (mainly the Talent Poolers), and guest shots played by shining lights like Marion Ross, Andrea Martin, Arte Johnson, Laraine Newman, Steve Franken and, reprising his Golden Age LT claim to fame, advertising and audio auteur Stan Freberg as the pathetic Pete Puma. (Oh, no. I've got alliterrhea!!) He was unavailable when Pete turned up as a janitor on "Tiny Toons," so I filled in, adding another classic LT to my resumé. When he returned to the role, there was a line echoing his from years ago, and I'm proud to say that my previous research allowed me to remind him to say, "But I *tink*" instead of "*think*"!! And Stan was grateful enough to say "Oh . . . Thanks. I mean 'Tanks.'"

Singing groups Boyz II Men and 'N Sync have both had the distinction of having done a music video with Sylvester and Tweety for promotional purposes. (Didn't meet? Right.)

My favorite episodes? Easy. I loved doing "Whatever Happened to Shorty Twang?" in which I also played a part based on Andy Griffith's gritty, ruthless rabble-rouser Lonesome Rhodes in *A Face in the Crowd*, a microscopic miscreant called Lonesome Roach!!

And we wrapped the series with a mind-warping yarn in which the cat finally eats that bird!! And it's not a trick ending!! (Yes, it is. Just kidding.)

First I met Friz. Then I was on Cloud 9 when Chuck Jones called me in for a visit!! He and his protégé, the spirited Stephen A. Fossati had devised a tribute to Mr. Freleng starring Sylvester. They'd storyboarded a theatrical short called *Father of the Bird* and needed the voice. I passed the test, and not only got my first chance to work with Chuck, but with June again too!! As the newborn bluebird who is alternately the object of his hungry desire and its protective parent, even her chirping of a single "Mama" identified her immediately and helped make this cartoon a modern landmark. It is that good, imho, but was released as an opener for WB's *The Man Who Knew Too Little*, which bombed. Dunno why this short is still unavailable to the public; everyone who's seen it has liked it — if not loved it — a lot.

I loved meeting Chuck's layout man and latter-day co-director, the artist Maurice Noble, at this short's WB screening. He struck me as a kindly old gent who spoke passionately about Chuck and their work together.

But before that, when the tracks were first finished, Steve arranged for Chuck and I to meet at his office on the lot. I brought a copy of his *Chuck Amuck* (which is still available) to sign. We discussed Fine Art more than anything, and in particular his favorite author and painter — Mark Twain and Marc Chagall.

I was fool enough to pun, "I guess you'd give 'em high marks, huh?"

To which he immediately replied, "Yeah, and they'd probably give me a "Hi, Chuck!!"

Now that's witty, kiddies, proof that the octogenarian was still sharp as a tack.

He was asked not to sign autographs anymore, however, to my distress, and someone was there to make sure of that. Adding his initials were the best he could do, and did so, apologetically. He closed the book and handed it back to me. Heavy of heart, I never even looked till after he died.

And then I discovered he had indeed written his full name in it!! Never one to obey unwanted restrictions, I took this mischievous practical joke on both his overseers (and me!!) as proof of his approval of my work, or worthiness of his famed signature — or "mark," if you will. And no one need worry: I'll never sell that book!!

Deliriously, that was only the beginning of my association with this living legend. The next project was to bring to life a series of online shorts he and Steve worked up, the misadventures of a know-it-all, hard-luck "TimberWolf." Thomas was his name, and this time I was hired to provide, not recycled Mel for a change, but an original voice!! Now I *felt* like Mel might've, though, having been issued this happy challenge!!

Chuck and Steve agreed that Thomas TimberWolf's character elements should combine a country gentleman's cracker-barrel drollery with a fatalistic view of his inevitable follies and fates, and come off kinda like an articulate Wile E. Coyote. A gang of woodland "friends" (nifty Nancy Cartwright, i.e.) only got in the way of this self-deluded loser's master plans. I set to work finding the best possible voice, or as close as I could get.

Being an impressionist, I knew that selecting a prototype from the vast pantheon of Western character actors might pay off, and simultaneously satisfy the audience's subconscious mindset of Thomas's vocal validity.

After reading the dialogue as Slim Pickens, Walter Brennan, Andy Devine, "Gabby" Hayes (my favorite Western actor ever), and many other sidekicks of note, I finally chose Chill Wills, a very talented Texan whose smug, easily-deflatable windbag characteristics fit Thomas like a paw in a glove. I didn't even have to affix much in the way of variations on his well-developed screen image. The director, Steve, and then Chuck, thought my selection perfect . . . and I love it when they use the "p" word!!

We did twenty "TimberWolf" episodes, and seventeen of them went webward. The first ones were supervised by "the man," and that made this a pet project for all of us.

We were ecstatic that our realization pleased him very much — especially in retrospect, since it was Chuck's last hands-on work in animation.

But, unlike other LT webworks, which you can catch on DVD releases like "Reality Check" and "Stranger Than Fiction," this series is, to date, another Jones treasure waiting to be rediscovered, though I'm 100% certain that time will accommodate him.

Yet, another project, in fact his final connection with the LTs, came to pass. *Daffy Duck for President* was another pet project (and he deserved ten more at least), one he'd had ready for years, based his book of the same name. Completed posthumously in 2004, much credit must also go to the Jones family, who helped see this film through.

A government-commissioned educational cartoon, his story explores — you guessed it: politics. But instead of raking the raucous rascal over the coals one more time, Chuck chose to instruct him (and student audiences) as to the basic structure of our democratic republic, and the process of getting a bill (to outlaw rabbits, predictably) passed. Bugs was his usual helpful self, Daffy obtuse as always, and I was deeply honored to have provided all the voices that Chuck, the cartoon, and classrooms needed.

This one has been made available for viewing on "Looney Tunes Golden Collection Volume 2." This short, which has a strong flavor of state-of-the-art Chuck, was helmed by Spike Brandt and Tony Cervone (who shall return shortly).

I surely, sorely miss my brief and only sporadic meetings and phone talks with Chuck.

Oh, to have been a fly on the wall during his, and his colleagues' ingenious glory days!! (Or should I say "a *termite in* the wall."..? Yes, I should say that.)

The climax of the ever-popular musicale "Bugs Bunny On Broadway" necessitated prerecorded voicework as well, though not much. Only a line or two. You could guess which one's the tagline, but I might as well tell ya. It's everyone's most requested Daffy line by a wide margin — "You're despicable!!"

So, yeah, I've done Broadway . . . !! — premiering on the Great White Way as Daffy, who has opened so many doors for me. And I subsequently enjoyed seeing and hearing myself as the most picayune but pungent part of this symphonic perennial at the Hollywood Bowl!!

The LTs have an historic link to good music, as do most Golden Age toons, and to weave that link into the fence sheltering Saint-Saens's *Carnival of the Animals* was a natural, and I've performed this variation twice so far!!

Once was at Pepperdine University, working with not only their student orchestra but with such fine co-stars as Obba Babatunde and the instantly lovable Kathleen Freeman. Younger generations know her irreplaceable face from *The Blues Brothers*, as the Mother Superior who sends them on their "mission from Gaahd," but I'm more partial to what she added to several of Jerry Lewis's best pictures!!

The second time around, at the family-friendly Starlight Bowl, I was invited to read a specially toon-tooled adaptation just this past Summer. As in Bob Clampett's *A Corny Concerto*, the emcee was Elmer Fudd, and they tell me I don't do too badly with this non-Mel LT. (What a wewief!!) And I can't think of too many of the WB menagerie who weren't on display. And I'm told we might do it again someday!! Hooray for Holl--!! er, Burbank.

Another career milestone was achieved when the two most famous LTs were asked to hand out the Best Animated Film award for the 1994 Academy Award ceremonies. Before helping Bugs name the winner, Daffy swooned over the stars in the audience. Sharon Stone was quite tittila– er, tickled pi– er, amused.

Trivia question: Which LT character has been in three Oscar-winning shorts, more than any other?

Answer: Sylvester!! (Now look up the titles yourself.)

To finish up with WB features for awhile, if you know your toons, you know I'm not in the voice cast of *Space Jam* (1996). In this case, I simply couldn't participate, for personal reasons. The film, starring Michael Jordan, and perpetuating the *Roger Rabbit* tradition of mixing animation with live-action (a much older tradition than that, as you undoubtedly know), did pretty well, despite most critics' questioning the wisdom of presenting hip-hop-style LTs. The new look didn't last long, at any rate.

At the very end of the century, however, I did many voices for *Tweety's High-Flying Adventure*, extrapolated from the "Mysteries" series. Kinda (exactly) like a musical *Around the World in 80 Days*, most of this direct-to-video feature works for me, including the high-quality score, traditional S&T humor, an exotic girlfriend for Tweety — and almost-constant TV reruns!!

Meanwhile, over at Disney, where I've seldom worked on the whole, I did enjoy a short spate of employment on two '90s series, doing small parts on "Bonkers" and a recurring comical villain for "The Little Mermaid"; the Lobster Mobster was a blustering, bullying burlesque of Edward. G. Robinson, ably abetted by David L. Lander as "Shrimp," and complete with clever, character-defining songs.

Even later, I was hired to be the ever-morphing voice of the Toon Disney channel, delivering two years' worth of daily promos before younger-sounding announcers became vogue. This was fun, non-stop work while it lasted, and was pervasively influential enough for my regular pipes to have been recognized one day by a four-year-old and his Dad during an elevator ride!!

Another famous duck fell into my lap in 1994, — and it hurt!! Not just a joke. What hurt was the fact that it didn't last very long.

The early '50s gave birth to a series starring a classic yet most unlikely animated star. Baby Huey, a literal "infant terrible," was featured in exactly eleven shorts (my lucky number). The gullible young giant was played by old comedy pro Sid Raymond, who also worked in sketches with . . . Jackie Gleason. (Weird but true. Even weirder: my mother's cousin directed the Florida show!!)

When my audition got me the job, I called Mr. Raymond, who was by this time retired and living in Florida. He was gratified to hear from me, and more than a little surprised that I knew his credits (which also included Paramount's longer-lived Katnip). Sid appreciated my questions about his career and my offering the occasion to pass the torch, however unofficially. And though the Harveytoons series wasn't renewed, it was an experience I thoroughly enjoyed and will always remember fondly.

That same year, the first installment of "Duckman" for Klasky-Csupo featured flashbacks to the title character's early life. Of course, Duckman had a Dad, and of course, he sounded like Yogi Bear. I'm still not sure what species that made him, but I did my best Daws Butler for him. The sarcastic show worked well, despite my paternal confusion, balancing better on the cutting edge than most.

Measurably more popular than that was K-C's "Rugrats," which I hardly needed to tell you, especially if you have kids. The premise of seeing the world through toddlers' eyes was as imaginative as TV fare gets, and everything fell niftily into place: sharp writing, ace direction and inspired acting meshed seamlessly, and is still proving successful in reruns after a decade on the air.

But then, the passing of the truly inimitable David Doyle, who'd been the beloved Grandpa Lou Pickles for seven seasons, led the show's makers to try and find a sound-alike. It was easier for me to approximate that uniquely fizzy voice (gruff and sweet, nasal and guttural, and funny and serious, all at the same time!!) than it was to equal the man's talent for just being his effervescent, true self. Mr. Doyle made it look easy, but he was an actor's actor, and millions of children's favorite babysitter.

So it was quite a chore for me to step into such big shoes, but they were comfy shoes too. And the wonderfully gracious K-C team, especially charming casting lady Barbara Wright, gave me a shoehorn. (I've switched to analogies now. Hope it's a better fit.)

They urged me to get as close as I could to David's performances, but also told me to make it my own and that this way, the casting change would attain an organic osmosis for even the most discerning ear. They were right; cast and crew, and fans and colleagues alike told me how smooth this transition felt to them!!

My first assignment was *The Rugrats Movie*, followed by two more features, and I continued in the role on TV and films till the end of the program's run. The cantankerous codger then appeared on "All Grown Up," its updated series about the same children's adolescence.

By the time "Rugrats" got its well-earned star on the Hollywood Walk of Fame, I no longer felt adopted by this fully functional family. Thanks, Barbara, Keith, Charlie Adler, Arlene and Gabor; plus cast regulars E. G. Daily, Christine Cavanaugh, Kath Soucie, Cheryl Chase, Jack Riley, Melanie Chartoff, Phil Proctor, Michael Bell, et al — for making me feel so at home.

And though Grandpa wasn't in every episode, picking favorites is difficult even among his own excursions. But I can tell you some of the ones I venerate most.

• "Hair!" - Very funny shaggy-senior story written by ex-stand-up colleague Monica Piper, with comedy stalwarts Ed Begley, Jr. and Tom Poston (as Lou's arch-rival McNulty).

• "Don't Poop on My Parade" Grandpa finds a girlfriend, Lulu, played by Hollywood honey Debbie Reynolds. (In real life, though, I dumped her.) / Sequel: "A Lulu of a Time"

• "Where's Grandpa?" - On a road trip, only the babies realize Grandpa's been left behind at a rest stop. What suspense!! Will Lou go over Niagara Falls in a barrel?!

- **"THE ART MUSEUM"** - Angelica takes the tots on an audio tour of "the Museum of Feaux Arts." Smart satire kids and adults alike can grasp. I like their spin on Ancient Egypt.

- **"BABIES IN TOYLAND"** - When Angelica searches for toys from Santa Claus, she finds the real meaning of Christmas instead. Lou is something of a hero in this holiday show.

- **"THE OLD AND THE RESTLESS"** - From "All Grown Up", this is my favorite show about the value of seniors, as sheer experience trumps the snide insults and rashness of youth.

My Dad, a Grandpa himself, tuned right into things, to my amused bemusement. He handed out my autographed "Grandpa Lou" photos by the dozens, never failing to elicit the happy surprise of hundreds of families he'd meet. Even more than what he called "the duck" and "the rabbit," this was the one that most made me a star in his eyes. For that, I'll always be grateful to Klasky-Csupo.

Chapter 17:
Well, You've Got to Star Somewhere

*A*rt Carney climbed the ladder to fame. Hank Azaria is doing the same even as we speak. But, ya know? Voice actors hardly ever get to star in movies. Hans Conried did once, starring in *The Twonky*. But these guys made an ongoing effort to break free from the mic.

Well, so did I, come to think of it. In 1988, I had my single shot at a feature film lead as risible Ron Douglas, a lighthearted but lovelorn lad of 36 years and 300 pounds who might literally become *Mr. Christmas Dinner* in the eyes of his hungry new girlfriend and her inbred family. Well, they say Hollywood can eat ya alive . . . !!

Pat Proft, co-creator of the "Police Squad"/*Naked Gun* TV show and features, penned this tenderized tale for the brand-new New Line Cinema, which changed the title to the not-as-specific *Lucky Stiff* before not releasing it. Wish *that* were a joke, but it went to no more than four or five middling markets before its rapid rescue via TV airings and wider videocassette circulation.

No, I'm not really bitter about it. The fledgling studio simply make a financial choice to throw their money behind their other late-year offering, the equally money-losing film version of Harvey Fierstein's prize-winning *Torch Song Trilogy*. In retrospect, maybe they shoulda just combined both plots and made everyone happy.

All joking aside, this movie was a joyride while it lasted. The director was none other than Hollywood icon Anthony Perkins, who, contrary to public image, was the sanest person on the set. At least as far as getting it done right. Most critics think it's not bad at all. It is strange, but most cannibal comedies are, aren't they? It's also loaded with choice dialogue, succulent artsy touches and one overbaked performance by yours truly. Well, what did ya expect from a ham but to sizzle on the burner?

I could write a separate book about this major cinematic event (in my life only, I guess), but let me start with the very able cast. It also stars adorable Donna Dixon, a very nice lady in real life, the impressive Jeff Kober, Brit wit W. Morgan Shepard, darling Fran Ryan, gung-ho Barbara Howard, and gaunt and brittle pro Bill Quinn.

Toonwise, as a tribute to my Looney origins, at one point I holler "Heeyahh, mule!!" to my team of horses loud and clear. Name that reference!!

Aw, Tony let me get away with murder, even allowing me to play it like Bob Hope — that is to say: with everybody playing it straight except me. But that's kinda the way it was written too. Anyway, it's a dark and foreboding holiday treat you wouldn't want to miss. And it is still available. I think. I dunno. It's a good, old-fashioned but very original, spooky comedy!! So go find it!! (Unless you decide to rent *The Twonky* instead.)

Making light of my one and only starring movie is unfortunately quite easy, but Tony Perkins, whose second and last film directing job this was, deserves more credit than I've given him so far. We endured some cold, snowy weather (Poor Bill Quinn!!) and major last-minute changes for a low-budget opus. Tony pulled it all together pretty damn well, if ya ask me. Not only that, he was personally everything you'd want a director to be, and then some: positive, open-minded and generous. Most of Hollywood only thought they knew him, but he wasn't really like Norman Bates, okay? Too bad he didn't get to direct more films. I'd bet he'd have bounced back with something even better!!

Hollywood publicists of yore used to roar that their product was likely to contain, "More stars than there are in Heaven!!!!" Well, Heaven's turned that score around by now, imho. But I've certainly met my share of greats, even though they may be an endangered species.

My definition of who is or was "great" may not be the usual roster of household names. But to me, this means "talented and accomplished." And I believe that in the future, true students of our culture will deem a Dabbs Greer or a Chuck McCann as important as a Gary Cooper or a Stan Laurel. Because there they are, as frequently and as impactful in their ways. And along my way, I noticed that, as the studio system rolled over and TV exploded into supernova, there were many such greats still working.

Everyone's ol' buddy Chuck McCann is one of these. His many impressive accomplishments aside, he understands the importance of keeping the Past alive in the Present. He and adroit comic actor Ronnie Schell helped fill the ranks of "Yarmy's Army," a friendship club of sorts named in honor of Don Adams's comedy writer brother Dick. Chuck and Ronnie both invited me come to one of their monthly dinners.

Actually, I asked to be invited, because I knew I knew I'd fit in. Glad they thought so too. And for someone like me, who knows a good deal of entertainment history, this was like walking into a customized dream.

At any given invitation-only dinner, one dined and chatted with the most loving, mutually supportive Show Biz greats, a flux of gifted and established writers, musicians, and other comedy contributors, as well as prominent actors and comedians as recognizable as Shelley Berman, Louis Nye and Phyllis Diller.

Even the famously guarded and hard-to-please Don Adams, Maxwell Smart himself, gave me a half-hour's conversation one night. And though he and others are gone now, they all had a great time respecting and taking care of each other. (Me too.)

I worked with blues monarch B. B. King, opening at his club up on Universal's City Walk. Watching him rehearse his group, I sang along to myself.

Then, during the break, he came over to me to say, "I heard you scatting. You oughtta do that for a living!!" — a great compliment. (I think . . . Or had he seen my act?)

I was one of many who did a live stand-up tribute show to Joe Pesci, produced by Judd Apatow, and was summoned to the recent Oscar-winner's box suite to deliver a private performance, by request, for him and his family. With *GoodFellas* still hot as a pistol, I think he liked the fact that I wasn't a bit scared of him!! (Well, he wasn't even trying to be funny that night.)

Here's another lucky encounter, and one that almost made me faint. But not for the reason you think . . .

The subject of this account was utterly unmistakable for absolutely anyone else. I walked into the same studio where I'd met Mel Blanc and saw this other archetypal giant of all media, including cartoon voicework, sitting on the couch, flanked by two attentive ladies. It was none other than that sly, slender, mop-headed Golden Ager, Sterling Holloway. That's not when I fainted. But I immediately lost all self-control, reverting to reverential amazement, knowing I was suddenly in the presence of a genuine "great"!! This was *Dumbo*'s stork!! The Cheshire Cat!! Uncle Oscar on "Superman"!! Et cetera, et cetera!!

I exclaimed, "Holy cow!! Hello, Mister Holloway!!"

At the same time, I noticed he also had a cane. And with visible effort, this gentleman — there is no other word — hoisted himself to his feet to greet — a stranger.

No, he couldn't know who I was. Yet this was not the point. He had been addressed in a way that told him he was known and loved, and responded accordingly, though the ladies he was with looked shocked and concerned.

That's when I felt a rush of guilty dizziness as I realized he shouldn't tax himself this way!!

But the ladies, his nurses as it turned out, also stood to support him by the elbows so he could shake my hand and thank me for thanking him for all his work. Like I was family, or an old friend, not just a fan.

Are you crying yet . . . ?

This was irrevocable proof to me of how Hollywood used to be, and how that aging dignity struggled to survive.

The words we spoke, whatever they were, paled in comparison to Mr. Holloway's second-nature demonstration of a more civilized culture.

Gone are those days, and people like him. I only hope Hollywood someday cyclically reclaims its former nobility, as personified for me by this meeting.

And let me mention in passing that Sterling Holloway also maintained his own art gallery.

And speaking of actors who had their own art galleries, (Neat segue, huh?!), here's the last of those anecdotal teasers, from way back in the first chapter yet!!

I did manage to meet one of my heroes of ham and horror: Vincent Price — totally by accident, and late in his life, in fact only a month before he died. But what a lucky encounter for me!! And of all places to meet him, it was in a supermarket!! The vegetable section yet!! Birthplace of Mr. Potato Head!!

As I shopped, I noticed a elegant, elderly fellow whose face was hardly hidden by an overhanging straw hat, seated in a wheelchair — and he was selecting a dripping head!! (of wet lettuce.) Recognizing the legendary actor at once, I approached another man standing nearby him, whom I recognized must be his valet. I asked this fellow if it would be all right to speak to Mr. Price, and it was, to my childlike joy, quite all right with my beaming idol!!

In this instance, I had to literally genuflect in order to converse with the now-frail, genial theatrical giant (but would have anyway, I think). I had a bookful of praise to offer, but knowing he'd heard it all before, I decided to keep our talk short and sweet to make it easy on him. But I felt ten years old again as that ol' black magic surfaced in his twinkling-eyed smile for one he could probably sense was a true and studied fan. (It's a fact that I'd seen almost all his films by then and all the TV work I could find. And told him so . . . I couldn't believe somehow he was now actually looking back at me!!)

What else did I say to him? I believe I mentioned my weaning on his Roger Corman budget-epics, told him he deserved an Oscar for *Champagne for Caesar*, *His Kind of Woman* and/or *Theater of Blood*, and thanked him for sharing his great sense of fun in just about every performance, even his best (non-hammy) ones, like *The Song of Bernadette*, *Laura*, *House of Usher* and *The Conqueror Worm*.

My reward was what must have been one of his last (if not his very last) autograph. I also had the unbridled temerity to do my impression of him *for* him -- though quietly, so as to avoid a stir amongst the other produce buyers. My Vincent proclaimed to the real one that he was going mad — mad!! — for a living!! — and that if this kept up, he'd go even madder!! (a later piece from my **stage act**.) He laughed. Yes, he genuinely laughed. And then *he* thanked *me,* shook my hand, and it was over. I walked away, unwillingly, yet grateful and thrilled that an ultimate goal of mine had been fulfilled: I had met Vincent Price, and for me it was a great experience!! Aside from his cinematic state of unending going-madness in the films I loved, who could fail to admire that he enjoyed a spotless reputation as a gentleman, and never lacked for work his whole life long? If I could have lived any actor's life in the twentieth century, his would be the one I'd choose.

And I'm afraid I'm not done with him yet!! (Sorry about the double-teaser, but it won't take as long to get back to him this time, I promise.)

Sure, I've bumped into lots of celebrities over time, sometimes accidentally on purpose — and sometimes, they've bumped into me.

WB was holding a recording session one day whereby the talent was "stacked," meaning they'd booked us in linear, one-at-a-time order, usually dictated by the actors' busy schedules. I sat and joshed with Ed Asner, whom I'd never met till that morning. He had already finished his work and said "g'bye" to me as I was summoned to the booth.

When I emerged, they told me Ed had sneaked in to watch me do my LT thing for a little while, then left.

A day or so later, to my surprise, he contacted me, and gave me his home phone number. Would Bugs and Daffy mind calling his young son to wish him Happy Birthday? Of course, I did just that. I never disappoint a kid if I can help it. So I called the Asners, granting his kid's every vocal request. Ed thanked me profusely, and we hung up.

And wouldn't ya know it? I saw him everywhere after that: at the studio, at various eateries, just everywhere.

So I couldn't resist stopping him the third time I spotted him jogging down a side street one day. I had the car pulled over in front of him, whereupon he stopped, breathless, and leaned on the open window.

"(Huff, puff) Joe . . . !! Thanks," he panted.

"For what? For calling on your kid's birthday?"

"No . . . (puff) . . . For stopping me . . . !!"

It's hard to make me laugh, okay? But he did.

Here's another Ed entirely.

One film I would love to have been in was Tim Burton's *Ed Wood*. But, to make a long, unintentionally funny story short, I couldn't get in the casting director's door. Not legitimately, since I was between on-camera agents at the time. So I stormed the joint!! Just like in old Hollywood movies *and* in real life, picture-and-resumé in hand, insisting I'd been talking about this guy and *Plan 9 from Outer Space* since the '60s. I felt like I somehow owed it to Ed to try to get into the thing, at least.

But this ploy didn't work. The casting person looked at me like I had two heads, didn't wanna hear my Orson Welles or anything else. And her casting board was crowded with still-open roles, but she invited me to just vamoose.

Oh, I know it was unprofessional of me to bypass the rules and beg. So I can't really blame her for tossing my pic-&-res into the wastebasket before my very eyes, can I?

But then, I said: "Future events such as these will affect you in the future." Then, all of a sudden, there were flying, flaming pie plates over Hollywood!! So Tor Johnson came in and hung me out a window by my collar!!

And then — !! I woke up . . . !! It all been a dream!! Just a crazy dream . . . (Okay, I'm done.)

The movie was better than my experience with it, thank goodness, although to me, perennial Burton star Johnny Depp seemed out of his dep' in the lead, with his cheeky, stylized performance. I woulda cast William Hurt.

Ed has a dream that he meets Orson Welles, his idol in this biopic, half-acted by Vincent D'Onofrio, who bears a striking resemblance. But I was struck more by the other half of this performance, — as voiced by Moe LaMarche!! Did Tim Burton really think that could fool *me?!* Hahahaha!! I couldn't wait to give Moe due credit for his fine, uncredited job of ADR. (Moe said Tim loved The Brain!!)

Anyway, the real star here was Martin Landau as Bela Lugosi — so good, he practically swept the whole world's awards for Best Supporting Actor that year.

While it was still in theaters, I met Mr. Landau in a restaurant parking lot. He was with his family, and just leaving, so I had to say whatever I was going to say fast!!

And it was sorta like meeting the man who became our universal Dracula himself, only funnier, probably.

If you think this man, this riveting actor (and fellow comedian portraitist) is anything less than a textbook pro, then get this: When I thanked him for raising good ol' Bela from the dead so vitally and poignantly, he said:

"Thanks!! Now go see *Pinocchio*!!"

— his next picture. A perfect Show Biz story, no?

Then there are the Ones That Got Away. I once spent ten minutes in a green room with the dazzling, underrated Gene Barry, shortly before "Burke's Law" returned to TV. Anxious as I was to meet him, just to say hi and thank him for that show and more, the producer he was working with saw me hovering and kept yapping away at Mr. Barry, circling to keep his back to me, purposely preventing me from even saying hello!! Of course, I could have chosen to be equally rude and interrupt, or push this guy out the basement window, but professionals must uphold decorum. And I was called into my session first. Damn!!

Well, since then I bought his autograph at a souvenir shop . . . And he's still working as of this writing . . . Maybe I'll send him a copy of this book and try again!!

While riding in an L.A. office building's elevator one afternoon, who should step in but Moses, General Andrew Jackson and Ben-Hur himself, the illustrious, charismatic, not-as-tall-as-I-thought Charlton Heston.

Now, elevator rides don't usually last long, but this was one minute I'll never forget. He didn't mind my button-holing him with a fast self-intro and "Thank you for *Touch of Evil* (another favorite since the '60s), in which he'd starred. He looked at me in a way that said he knew what

I really meant. And he was right. I wasn't complimenting his performance, but his wisdom.

He told me it was simple logic. He'd heard that his male co-star would be Orson Welles, and that no director had been assigned yet by Universal. So he picked up the phone and recommended him strongly for the job. And in retrospect, he was proud to have had the influence to do so, adding "It's probably the best contribution I've ever made to the cinema."

"Offscreen," I smiled.

Then the doors parted, and, shaking hands, so did we.

Hey, I'd been telling folks about that movie since the mid-'60s, (not unlike my enthusiasm about *Plan 9*), long before its restoration(s) and acceptance into the ranks of world classics!! And it wouldn't have gotten there without Mr. Heston. So we both felt kinda validated, ya know?

Right after that, I walked into an audition and sat next to another remarkable actor from Orson's last Hollywood magnum opus. Dennis Weaver said he'd been new to films, and true to his onscreen type, felt nervous about working with the man who'd made *Citizen Kane*. Welles told him he was to be the "Shakespearean fool" of the story and wanted him to go all-out, to be crazy, that nothing would be too much. The young Mr. Weaver was fearful that the director's vision might earn him a reputation as a ham — no kidding — but *"I believed!!"*

"And delivered the goods," I chimed in.

"Well, thanks. But it was all his idea. I just followed direction. And what a lucky guy I was to have that chance to work with him on that."

If you've seen this movie, and this extraordinary performance, you'll appreciate that the real Dennis Weaver, more than thirty years later, still felt humble and grateful for that auspicious opportunity.

Even more mind-boggling, in a much different way, was something that happened one night as I cabbed home from the Improv. Speaking of Orson Welles, which I'd just been doing with someone, I learned that his favorite haunt was the Ma Maison restaurant, now-defunct.

On a whim, I asked the driver to take me there, in the hope of finding the great man alone and amenable to any access. But neither of us knew where it was, so I just went home . . .

Twenty-four hours later, I shivered as I read the incredible headline: Orson Welles had died that same night, — after dining at Ma Maison . . . !!

Am I psychic? I dunno. But it's also true that a week before Christmas in 1977, I drew and lithographed a portrait of Charlie Chaplin, had them framed and handed them out as presents to my family.

Yep, you guessed it: the page-one story of his death *the day before* was an eerie complement to this uncannily apt set of gifts!! Mom, Dad, brother and sister gave me rather wide berth for the rest of the holiday.

And to this day, I —

Omigosh!! I just realized I drew cartoons of myself all over this book!!

Chapter 18:
Meanwhile, Outside the Looney Bin...

The title of this chapter refers to v/o work I did for cartoons other than the LTs. And that was the most boringly functional sentence I've *ever* written.

Hey, listen: Voice acting can be very demanding, even exhausting if you happen to do Daffy all day!! But then there are times when something like this happens:

The show was "Ally McBeal." I was contracted to give them the voice of "Mr. Ed" (TV's talking horse, not Messrs. Asner or Wood) for a nightmare sequence. But for me it was a most pleasant, dreamlike experience.

I was driven to the lot and immediately met by an assistant who escorted me to the sound stage, opened the door and loudly announced my arrival:

"Joe Alaskey's here!!"

Some of the cast were present, and they and all of the crew stopped what they were doing and turned to watch my entrance as I was led to a tall director's chair in the center of the set.

"Jeeze," I thought. "These people are really organized!!"

Asked to sit, I sat. Instantly, a boom mic descended into place, six inches from my nose.

"People?" a voice rang out, obviously the director. "This is Joe Alaskey, our Mister Ed."

"Really organized!!" I'm thinking.

Polite applause from my sudden audience. The assistant handed me my "sides" (script pages; one page in this case). I looked over my material and saw it was a simple verbal gag at Ally's boyfriend's expense. Real easy stuff.

"Ready, Joe? Can you give us a test?" I said my first line. "Great. Okay. Let's do it."

The lights dimmed, though I don't know why, except for a wide spot over my shoulder so I could read.

"Quiet, please . . . Okay, Joe."

Strikingly toplit, I read my two or three lines once, then I read them again for "safety." Then they taped twenty or so seconds of "room tone" (silent ambiance) to lay all their v/o tracks over, and then:

"Okay, we're good. Thank you, Joe."

More applause. Up come the lights. I hop out of the chair, and here's the assistant with the paperwork for me to sign; she starts walking me out. And as I swiftly exited, out of the corner of my eye I glimpsed whom I think was Callista Flockhart standing, arms akimbo, watching me with an expression that said, "How do ya like this guy?! Maybe I'm in the wrong business!!"

Seeing this, I almost lost it. I couldn't have imagined a smoother, faster operation, or a funnier finale to this adventure in recording. Whoever she was, I hope that young lady finds Life as easy as I did that day!!

I enjoyed similar star treatment on other shows like "Everybody Loves Raymond", and many of them worked with similar speed and efficiency.

For "Fresh Prince of Bel Air," I did Bob Hope's voice for a golf course gag (later cut), and got to meet Will Smith, who was just arriving as I left. Having seen the show, I gave this capable newcomer some encouraging words, and he was quite pleased to collect my vote of confidence.

Back on camera, I had a blast on the sitcom "Nurses," starring my seasoned stand-up colleague, Jeff Altman. And what a plot!! In "Eat Something," a "Star Trek" convention has been hit by food poisoning, and its attendees go to the hospital in varying stages of internal distress. I played one of several costumed fans (What's the word for them?) who can't stop emulating their favorite characters!! I was the ersatz Captain Kirk (who hallucinates being William Shatner). The lines were screamingly funny as the Trekkers (There ya go.) sank deeper into their shared illness and delirium, even planning to take over the facilities!!

The climax was my confrontation with poker-faced Florence Halop, whose character cruelly burst the "Captain's" bubble of unreality. Dropping the Shatner act at last, my character ended up sneering at her, "If we ever need a Klingon, I'll give you a call!!"

To really rub it in to you Trekkers, I gotta brag that we were actually allowed to use the original "communicator" and "phaser" props, right outta the museum, for a week!!

Wish I'd had more parts like this. But, dammit, Jim, I'm a Ham, not an guest star!!

Two more '90s commercials I did on-camera are worth mentioning, I suppose.

Sega had me as a confused Dad wandering around a typical department store at Christmastime, trying to remember their product name. "Saga? Saygo? Siggy?"

And I wound up as a hospital patient whose wife and kids bring him homemade cookies, while a guy in a "Full Body Cast" suffers terribly, unable even to answer the burning question, "Got Milk?" That spot ran for years!!

Dunno why I waited so long to mention it, but I worked almost a whole year on Universal's major '95 film release, the live-action-and-animation *Casper*.

Hotshot director Brad Silberling's first feature, the kidflick was produced by Steven Spielberg, starred the magnanimous Bill Pullman, enchanting Cathy Moriarty, and young Christina Ricci, who falls for the boy phantom.

Using a variation on Golden Age toon voice Frank Graham (WB's *Hamateur Night* emcee and Tex Avery's bootie-booting "George"), I energized his slow, nasal delivery, nastied up his attitude, and got the role of Uncle Stinkie.

Casper himself was the voice of Malachi Pearson; his ghostly trio of uncles were played by Brad Garrett (as the booming Fatso), Joe Nipote (our squeaky-voiced Stretch), and snarky, smelly me. Side by side for months on the set, Joe, Brad and I were made an organic part of the movie-making process. It was a welcome change for me not to just put behind a soundproofed window, and I enjoyed this change of pace immensely, though it was a long and complicated shoot for all concerned.

We got to work with the unbelievable effects wizard Dennis Muren, perfectionist cinematographer Dean Cundey, and a whole team of experts throughout.

We ghosts were sent to ILM, George Lucas's workshop in San Francisco, and had little bitty lights pasted all over our faces to capture facial expressions, the good ol' rotoscoping process (you know — animating over live film), which worked seamlessly to humanize the ethereal.

Inevitably, as he'd done for us on "Tiny Toons," Mr. Spielberg himself ("Steven, please!!") visited his project.

Well, he did more than that, to my astonishment.

There was a scene near the end wherein Casper, flying around town, trying to find his new girlfriend, invades the TV set of a typical Dad. Steven tested me and suddenly, I had two parts in this movie!! Since Uncle Stinkie looked nothing like me, this would work fine as long as I used a different voice. So Steven personally directed me in this vignette, exercising his directing muscles and general prerogative. He had me slumped back in an easy chair, wearing a baseball cap. When Casper popped in accidentally, he pulled the cap brim down over my eyes to prevent me seeing a g-g-g-ghost, and I did a what-wuzzat take.

That was it. Don't recall that scene? Right you are. This bit was cut for being too extraneous to the mounting denouement. Hey, no hard feelings. These things happen all the time. And it was so short, we did it within thirty minutes, I think. And I'm truthfully content to say that I was once directed by this great filmmaker.

One minor disappointment: Despite my casting as that Dad, the uncles were to have been seen as their predeceased selves for one sequence that was also cut along the way!! (Drat!! We really dug our Gay Nineties costumes!!)

The public and most critics ate *Casper* up, food fights, ectoplasmic puppy love and all, and the saturation marketing was quite spirited — and very friendly!! (Two exceptionally appropriate puns . . . You're welcome.)

Eep!! I almost forgot to mention the series spinoff. Lasting two years and earning an Emmy along the way (for what, I forgot), it was fun to do and welcome income, but nothing special, to tell the truth. Unless you love these characters, um, to death.

Did I mention Nickelodeon? No? Why not? I've done lots of guest voices for them on a fairly regular basis, audible on episodes of "Johnny Bravo" and "Oh Yeah! Cartoons" as various fringe and one-shot characters; and "My Life as a Teenage Robot," as Eye-van, an evil alien eye who sounded like my best Claude Rains.

I also fill in from time to time for the illustrious Ernest Borgnine as Mermaid Man in "SpongeBob SquarePants" computer games. (This squeaky-piped senior superhero isn't all that easy to do; Borgnine's sharp as ever.)

I began my association with Cartoon Network when they aired the WB short *Carrotblanca*, which just missed the mark imho, not to mention *Casablanca*'s anniversary a year earlier. Hey, it's all . . . . timing, ya know?

But by 2003, WB would be working directly with for CN, on a show which may be their best ever. Yeah, I think so . . . And yeah, I'm in it. Wanna make somethin' out of it, buddy? Okay, it's terrific in spite of me, if you prefer. But hold on. I'll get there in a minute.

I did episodes of CN's frenetic "Time Squad," as several characters from history, including Wilbur Wright, Samuel F. B. Morse and Robin Hood (my tribute to Daws Butler's oft-heard David Niven take-off).

CN's Adult Swim bloc also put me to work in "Harvey Birdman," a show about a superhero/attorney with basic human problems. I didn't help him out much as a guy who calls himself Fear One (my rendering of Don Messick's shrill sickie), or as Peter Potamus, who kids him a lot in the men's room, — in my voice?! Teams of cryptologists are still slaving away to find out what's really going on here.

But my favorite for CN was "Samurai Jack" (episode VII). In this I was invited by vivacious v/o director and dynamite lady Collette Sunderman to play the dramatic roles of a scarred, yarn-spinning (and kinda hammy) general, and a soulful alien guardian in this highly abstract, world-class series that I still consider one of the best animated programs to ever hit the airwaves.

Around the mid-'90s, I found that the work I was getting behind the mic had become so frequent and time-consuming, I decided to retire from stand-up and on-camera acting — though now I feel ripe for a comeback.

Hm? What do they call it now? Oh. "Reinvention."

Well, with a nutty, unpredictable livelihood like mine, I wouldn't be surprised if I ended up playing a robot in commercials for Pterodactyl Helper on planet Neptune.

But while I've been ruminating on my future since I became invisible, there's been plenty of Looney Tunes work to do.

Chapter 19:
The Day My Pants Fell Off in Public, or: Names Aren't All I Drop

*O*kay, I lied. I worked on-camera a little.
I did that TV movie about Ali.

And I and can be seen wearing too much makeup but some nice clothes in interviews connected to WB product like the "Looney Tunes Golden Collection Volume One." Knock yourself out finding me on those discs while you enjoy the classic cartoons that Chuck Jones told us they made not for kids, not for adults, but for themselves, and which are fortunately still available to us all.

In 1996, one of my more unusual missions as Daffy entailed two very interesting firsts. First, it was all CG (computer-generated), and second — it was my first whack at doing Duck Dodgers, DD's sci-fi hero alter ego. Eye-popping effects stole the show, though Marvin the Martian (also articulated by me) worked well animated this way (better than the duck), his skittering walk being effectively applicable to this then-relatively-new process.

And instead of playing in theaters, the German-funded *Marvin der Martian in der Dritten Dimension* helped launch WB's flagship merchandise emporium in NYC, where it played on the second floor for years. Though the nationwide chain eventually dissolved, I thought it was a pretty shrewd move using a toy store as its playhouse. (Get it? Sorry.)

Meanwhile, in Cleveland, Ohio, Daffy Duck visited the offices (and set) of "The Drew Carey Show."

The everyman star is a real nice guy, I must say, though his comic self and the little black duck didn't exactly get along in the pre-title sequence of that show's season finale, "My Best Friend's Wedding."

On the pretext of seeking employment, Daffy sprayed everything with his wettest lisp, angrily charged Drew with discrimin-imin-ation, stole a kiss from Kathy Kinney's Mimi and, upon realizing he was only in another kind of cartoon, ended up wrecking the joint!!

Gerry Cohen directed this unexpected homage to the crazy-darnfool duck (not Chuck's greedy loser) with a sure hand and a robot janitor.

As the world entered the new millennium, the LTs seemed to be sailing through creative doldrums, but that wouldn't last very long.

WB greenlighted another toons-meet-the-real-world epic all their own in 2002, *Looney Tunes Back in Action*. (What, no punctuation? Nope.)

TV animation writer-producer Larry Doyle ("Daria"; "The Simpsons") pitched the premise of our title toons helping a fired WB security guard, Brendan Fraser, rescue some indescribable maguffin and his superspy father Timothy Dalton from evil, wacky Acme mogul Steve Martin, with the help of gradual love interest Jenna Elfman. I'm not sure if this was the original plot, because I wasn't involved at first. But that's the way it came out. From the get-go, it was rumored that the story, script and entire project were going through myriad, expensive changes. Before too long, Mr. Doyle was no longer active in his own project, though he retained a co-producer and sole writing credit.

Many months into production, it was decided that key v/o talent should be replaced. Auditions were reconsidered and I finally made the grade, now cast as both LT leads, and a measured handful of other characters.

Ultimately, I played heroes Bugs Bunny and Daffy Duck, plus Sylvester, Beaky Buzzard and Mama Bear, though throughout the process of finishing this film, I could never be sure who I'd be by the end credits.

Determined director Joe Dante, whose animation and comedy chops certainly made him the best qualified man to helm this movie, had his hands full already trying to pull things together as I stepped aboard.

He carefully led me through the arduous process of re-recording old dialogue and reams of new stuff; sometimes the ink on my sides was literally still wet!! And due to daily modifications from many new writers and rewriters, this picture definitely holds my career record for sheer numbers of sessions, let alone line changes!!

It was not an easy job for any of us to do, and not having a full script to refer to (few people did), I began to wonder if this thing would ever get off the ground!!

Week after week, ace animator Eric Goldberg helped Joe voice-direct me, and ended up doing fragments of Daffy and Bugs voicework himself. That's him as Bugs in the somewhat arbitrary *Psycho*-swipe shower scene, for instance. And when I saw the movie, I realized he'd also assumed the roles of Tweety Bird, Marvin the Martian and Speedy Gonzales (best of the three), vocally outdoing his mentor Richard Williams by two classic cameos. Anyway, Eric's one hard-working guy, and, frankly, I hope he sticks to animation from now on.

Also surviving the casting calamities on this frantic film: jocular Jeff Glen Bennett as Foggy, Sam and Nasty Canasta; Bob Bergen as Porky (Nobody else can do him like Bob!!); Casey Kasem and Frank Welker as Shaggy and Scooby Doo; Will Ryan (one of the good guys) as Papa and Stan Freberg as his ageless Junyer Bear (listed as "Baby"); vigorous, versatile Danny Mann; Mel Blanc's inimitable car noises; and as Granny, as ever, good ol' Junie-wunie!!

Egad!! I almost forgot: I was there when Brendan Fraser (a fine actor and a big kid, ladies and gentlemen.) tried out for -- and got -- the part of the Tasmanian Devil(s)!!

Anyway, even with so many cooks stirring the broth in so many directions for so long, the movie wound up being rather watchable, I think.

Unfortunately, the promotional budget had become more limited by this time. As a result, *LTBIA* only enjoyed a short release, even in major cities.

Yet despite these setbacks, we did pretty well at the box office for as long as it was out there, amassed mostly favorable reviews, and I became convinced me that Joe Dante is some kinda unsung genius. His trademark cameos alone were worth paying money to see: Roger Corman, Kevin McCarthy, Mary Woronov, Ron Perlman and Ro-Man (*Robot Monster*)!! Not to mention Golden Age Hollywood's gangster supreme Marc Lawrence!!

The kicker of all this for me was when we got reviewed by "Ebert & Roeper." Here's what Chicago cinecritic Richard Roeper said, quote, "Special mention has to go to Joe Alaskey, who honors the late Mel Blanc with his uncanny characterizations of Bugs, Daffy, Tweety [sic], and a host of other animated favorites. Thumbs up," unquote. Wow, thanks again, man!! And Roger Ebert concurred thumbwise, adding that *LTBIA* "has a nice, goofy charm about it."

Well, who doesn't love the Looney Tunes?

The Aflac duck might give ya an argument, even if he never gets the chance, as usual. For the spot co-starring Bugs and Daffy, again someone cast me as both LT VIPs, atypical of my TV exposure in general. I also liked the fact that another duck falls off the cliff for once!!

Hot on the heels of *LTBIA*'s relative success zoomed "Duck Dodgers"!! Of the 24th-and-a-half Cent-u-ryyyy!!

This was a series just itching to happen. Spike Brandt and Tony Cervone formulated a series for WB based on Chuck Jones' and Mike Maltese's glorious 1953 short. Nobody who's seen it can ever forget it, and the space opera genre typically allows for a huge variety of imaginative stories.

And the scripts were mostly good-to-excellent!! By 2003, the characterizations, plotting and dialogue would follow well-known lines. As we started, we could all kinda guess how it would play. And yet, Spike and Tony managed to throw some unexpected and hilarious, and even witty curves.

Honored again to play both Daffy and Marvin (bad good guy and good bad guy) in their guises of Dodgers and Commander X-2 (using his original name), I was just as happy to be working again with Bob Bergen's Porky (Eager Young Space Cadet), plus a spiffy cast of regulars: down-to-earth, talented temptress Tia Carrera as the love-starved Martian Queen; Michael Dorn, a "Star Trek" alumnus and basso profundo funster as a whole army of self-serving Martian robots; and Richard McGonagle, equally first-rate with straight and comic material as the insecure, banana-scarfing, spacy space boss, Dr. I. Q. High.

Spike and Tony storyboarded, wrote and directed the two-story shows themselves, assisted by distinguished animavens Mark Banker, Paul Dini and Tom Minton. And voices were truly fine-tuned by aforementioned voice director Collette Sunderman. The classic Jonesian design and animation was inarguably right-on, and computer-generated effects for outer space scenes were dazzling.

WB's Sander Schwartz and Cartoon Network exec Sam Register made it all happen. Along with sweet, omnipresent producer Bobbie Page, they guaranteed the highest possible standards of quality for "DD," and got a cartoon series classic in return!! What a team!!

If I sound more enthusiastic about this program than other WB stuff, — Well, you're right!! I can't help it!! The concept, the look and feel of it, and the big-kid appeal to me *personally* have made it my favorite LT endeavor to date!!

And what earnest, consistent homage to Chuck Jones and Mike

Maltese!! I'm positive that both of them really would've been proud of this series.

In fact, I love it so much, I'm going to list a lot of my favorite episodes!! (And I'll try to keep my customary double-exclamation points to a minimum.)

Ready? Here goes!! (Oops.)

• "Duck Deception" spins romantic farce to the nth degree. Dodgers forces the Cadet to woo Commander X-2 in drag, while he attempts to steal the Martian's energy core. Bob's best showcase, imho, as he grows comfy in his disguise.

• "The Fowl Friend" is a parody of "The Iron Giant," every bit as touching, but with more than a touch of ironic self-mockery. Outstanding is Kevin Michael Richardson as the basically human Agent Roboto, your real star here.

• "Duck Codgers" rapidly turns our heroes old, and their nemesis into . . . Baby Marvin!! Uproarious and unexpectedly tender observation of the aging process, which changes nothing really in anyone's personalities.

(aired with —)

• "Where's Baby Smartypants?" spanks the intellect as a babysitting chore becomes a bumptious chase when X-2 kidnaps the axiom-spouting, infant peacemonger. This is a perfect ensemble piece graced with a trenchant punchline.

• "The Wrath of Canasta" recalls the clever cinethriller "Westworld," adding a classic Jones baddie and side-splitting sagebrushed lingo, tunefully tweaked by the tangy, twangy Riders in the Sky. Just plain funny, pardner.

(aired with --)

• "**They Stole Dodgers' Brain**" explores the irresistible premise of DD as a well-adjusted genius, thanks to his 'great new hat.' Maybe our wittiest work, with Richard McGonagle's I. Q. High at his comical best.

• "**I'm Gonna Get You, Fat Sucka**" has the Cadet as the target of a lugubrious lard-vampire, while Dodgers is hypnotized into a combination of Peter Lorre and Renfield. Enormously entertaining situational gags and dialogue.

(aired with —)

• "**Detained Duck**" presents the duck's doppelganger, Drake Darkstar, a virulently evil escaped con. But who's really worse? Favorite line of series: "You sold his sister to a sausage factory? Dude, that's cold!!" Ed Asner guest stars.

• "**The Queen Is Wild**" highlights Tia's willful monarch as she pursues caddish, conceited DD, while lovelorn Marvin and incredulous Cadet moan for different reasons. Her last scene recalls a memorable line from another Jones classic.

• "**The Green Loontern**", a two-parter (one whole show): This DC Comics-inspired epic has DD join the superhero gang when he picks up the wrong outfit at his dry cleaners. The writing is a topnotch tribute to its source, and guest stars John Delancie, Kevin Smith and Hanna-Barbera's venerable voice vet John Stephenson really enrich the fun.

- "ENEMY YOURS" offered me a third role as Dr. Woe (née J. Evil Scientist, now with intentional Vincent Price pipes), whom DD tries to impress as a worthy adversary, with Commander X-2, as ever, equally unimpressed.

And this was only the first season!!

As we were about to wrap, Bobbie informed Bob Bergen and I that WB was making submissions to ATAS for Emmy consideration, and that we were among them. The category: Outstanding Performer in an Animated Series.

How nice!! Often an actor makes his or her own bid, but there's probably more oomph when the studio gets behind you. I was flattered but doubtful of my chances.

I'd been previously promoted for Plucky's first TTA season, but was aced out by five much better-known names.

Now all I was asked to do was suggest which show I thought my best. My work as Marvin could not be included in their submission; the Duck was on his own, unless I wanted to make a separate bid myself. That might actually bisect any chance I had, I thought, so I decided not to do that.

I picked "The Wrath of Canasta"/"They Stole Dodgers' Brain", figuring this one was truest to the Daffy/Dodgers character itself, sans vampiric or villainous variations.

Bob and I were working at the Kodak Center, where the ceremonies would be held months later, when he told me the 2003-'04 nominations were out, and I was in. Unfortunately, he wasn't. And I was speechless. Except for telling Bob it'd have been more fun if he'd gotten a nod himself.

The other nominees deemed deserving were: Nancy Cartwright (Bart on "The Simpsons") for a Disney show, Walter Cronkite (for PBS, as Benjamin Franklin on "Liberty Kids"), John Ritter (as "Clifford the Big Red Dog"), and Henry Winkler ("Clifford's Puppy Tales"). Wow. Big time competition. But 'competition' is a misnomer in this case; none of us campaigned, as far as I know.

All I could say for two days was, "I'm up against Walter Cronkite?! You gotta walk by his full-size statue to enter the TV Academy!!" But was I intimidated? Well, yep.

And then, as a NATAS member, I was in the weird position of deciding to vote for myself or not. I know if I did, the person opening my secret ballot would think, "Huh. Egomaniac." Always doing homework, I checked out the other nominees, and found Henry Winkler's work excellent and full of heart. Great. Now I was torn between desire and guilt!!

Then, Fate stepped in. Shortly after the nominees were announced, John Ritter, one of the best all-around comic actors of the latter 20th century, died suddenly, tragically far too soon.

Shocked and saddened, as everyone was, I couldn't help thinking that this would affect the final tally.

And everybody agreed with me, including Mom, who warned, "Don't get your hopes up," so my feelings wouldn't be hurt. It did seem inevitable that he would win posthumously. By this time, I was even hoping for it, for his family's sake. Wouldn't you?

Who did I vote for? Guess . . . !! (I'm not the kind to vote and tell.)

Then Bob and I were invited to be presenters for some of the other animation awards, and had fun customizing our material to Captain-and-Cadet byplay. Spike, Tony and others there wished me good luck, but with similar, near- maternal caution. At least I looked good in my retro tux, which made me feel like the Ambassador of Wackyland.

I saw Ellen DeGeneres and company before the show, reminded her of the Tahoe gig and "Lassie," and wished her luck with her first Emmy experience. (And her show won a bunch of stautuettes.)

The show was 19 hours and 88 minutes long when my category

came up. Someone told me to stand close to the stage entrance, just in case. Oh, well. Bob and I had to finish our bits anyway. A soap actor read the names. I put the cap back on my bottled water, — and won the award!!

I got light-headed, having come this close to doing a spit-take, and bounded to the dais in disbelief!!

I thanked everybody on the show, the other nominees, plus Bill & June, Mike Maltese, Chuck Jones, Mel Blanc, Sander, Eddie O. Collins (our unbeatable engineer), family, friends, and who knows who else. I'd have to see the tape they gave me. But I'm superstitious. With my luck, I might not win twice in a row.

Anyway — Applause!! Photos!! Pats on the back!! More photos!! My niece Trish was radiant with more than her natural beauty. I called Mom long distance.

"Mom!! Guess what?! I won!!"

A pause, then, "Whattya *mean* you *won?!*"

I laughed, reminded of Yogi Berra.

"Hey, I don't know *what* I mean, y'know what I mean? But I just won the award!!"

Everyone I know was flabbergasted, none more so than I, with congratulations from all.

Some interesting facts: No major award had ever covered voice actors in Mel's lifetime, though he surely deserved one. And after five Oscars for Sylvester, Tweety, Pepe LePew, Speedy, and Bugs, this was Daffy's first accolade for anything. I still find it amazing that a sentimental vote for John Ritter didn't come to pass, and that all-time loser Daffy Duck finally won (something, anything)!! Just as he would've wanted, and insisted, under normal circumstances, of course.

What made me feel just as good as winning was the fact that, I later realized, I didn't have to lift a finger to win this award (which has usually gone to much more famous names than mine)!!

Strangely (imho), however, "Duck Dodgers" didn't win anything else that night. For Outstanding Animated Program, I myself had to announce another surprise winner, the tween-marketed "Tutenstein". Hope I kept a straight face, because, frankly, I thought "DD" was miles above the choice of this creepily coy and cloying contrivance.

Shortly thereafter, DD's second and third seasons were combined, most of them airing on Cartoon Network before it was given to its little brother network Boomerang, where it's played twice a day or more ever since.

High standards of quality remained intact for the rest of our run, with several stories earning my highest recommendation, if that still means anything to you:

- "CASTLE HIGH" endeavors to explain how Dodgers wrecked his boss's ancestral home in about thirty seconds. A shaggy dog story with a *Young Frankenstein*-type monster, school-kids and angry villagers unravels. Very amusing, with more fine, fusty fuming from McGonagle's bent straight man.

- "JUST THE TWO OF US" pits DD and the Martian Commander against each other in a silly study of survival and frustration. Michael Dorn exhibits his incisive comic timing as his multicharacter robot-guards enjoy a vacation with the Cadet and a team of bikini-clad student nurses.

- "SURF THE STARS" features one of our greatest living songwriters, Brian Wilson, as an ethereal version of himself advising surfing king Dodgers how to win his beach brawl with the Crusher, played with gusto by John DiMaggio.

(aired with —)

- **"Samurai Quack"**: One of our all-time best, a none-too-gentle ribbing of guest star Genndy Tartakovsky's "Samurai Jack" (which you already know I loved), complete with the eminent Mako as DD's ultra-evil alarm clock. "Behold —!! my messy hair of determination!!"

- **"Talent Show a Go Go"** stages a voice-switcheroo between Dodgers and the singer of the show's theme song, none other than Tom Jones (no relation to Chuck), and hilarity ensues.

I mean that; the laughs are solid and non-stop. And who knew the swinging Welshman could be so funny?

Other guest stars for this extended season included TV's Ed McMahon in a neat self-parody; the astute George Takei (Mr. Sulu of "Star Trek", natch); Kelly Ripa (whom I didn't get to meet); singer Macy Gray (ditto); monologist Lewis Black (ditto) and "Macho Man" Randy Savage (ditto; but all they matched the show's spirit snappily); a watchful, eager-to-please Quentin Tarentino; and a friendly Henry Winkler. (I remembered him as a contemporaneously starving actor in NYC. And I'm happy to tell you he won the Emmy award in that same category the next year.)

I'll stop here. You get the point. This may be the best cartoon series WB has aired since the classic LT packages of the '60s.

"Yes, and all because of me!!"

Oh, shut up, Daffy. (Gosh, what a pompous jerk. He even stuck a little hard-rubber figurine of himself inside the statuette's upraised globe!!)

As for more Emmys, no thanks. It *is* a gamble. And I'm not the type who goes after awards anyway. Knowing that good work will survive is reward enough. Besides, that same Academy person is probably still opening the ballot envelopes . . . !!

Last word: I miss doing "Duck Dodgers" like crazy. Rumor has it that WB will puts us on DVD, and let's all hope that's soon.

Okay, so what was that about my pants falling down? Was that a figure of speech?

Um, no . . . !! I meant that literally!! Here's what happened: I was performing live in public and my pants fell down. Satisfied?

No? Sigh. Well, if you *must* have details . . .

It happened at a live promotional event for the release of the first "Golden Collection," a media event. WB asked if I would speak off-stage for the costumed characters who would interact with the invited audience (lots of families with little kids). My handheld mic was positioned behind the audience, but in relatively plain sight —

Scared yet? No?

— right next to the paparazzi.

Now you're scared. But I wasn't. We got along fine.

Pants-wise, here's the deal: I had lost some weight but hadn't invested in any svelte new vestments yet.

And then (choke!!) Foghorn Leghorn betrayed me!!

As I inhaled mightily to deliver a typically windy Foggy line, — Ker-plop!!

It got a lot windier all of a sudden.

But even this incredibly awkward distraction wasn't embarrassing enough — Foggy had more to say . . . !! Another few sentences, in fact!! Yeesh!!

All I could do was keep talking as I reached down and worked them back up my still-ample frame as best I could!! One-handed!! I had to keep holding the mic — *and* the copy I was reading!! Kids, try this at home sometime. Just get in plenty of practice before you go out and find a crowd.

Wait, now — Here's the real payoff: As my trousers hit the floorboards, the ever-alert paparazzi turned as one, eyes wide with wonder and purpose —!!

But instead of showering me with snaps of shutters and ejected

166   "That's _Still_ Not All, Folks!!"

light cubes, these guys actually formed a wall, and, with their backs to me, took not one picture, but allowed me to finish my terrible task, now completely blocking the audience from watching!!

Surprised? I was!! They sacrificed a cheap gag photo for charity's (not to mention society's) sake. No one ever saw this clothing calamity but them!!

Later, I just had to ask one of the pro shutterbugs why they not only spared, but saved my — um, saved me. He said they liked me because I'd given them all the time for pix and interviews an hour or so earlier. Whoa, I'd forgotten all about that!! Aha. Good karma had returned, and I was most grateful.

But, sorry, I shall never disclose whether it's boxers or briefs.

The real punchline: Next morning, Sander Schwartz messengered me a pair of Bugs Bunny suspenders. With a suitably sarcastic sympathy/gift card.

Before I wrap up my Looney Tunes tales for good, there's one other person I'd like to acknowledge. The one person who's been there on every major job I've done for WB is ADR Recording Editor Kelly Ann Foley.

How this adorable, hard-working lady has put up with even looking at me through the double-window these past twenty years is beyond me, and she is worthy of a very honorable mention. Anyway, she laughs. And I'm very grateful for just that much.

Chapter 20:
Who Said 'You Can't Go Home Again'?

Thomas Wolfe (not he of the Timber genus) once said, "You can't go home again . . ."

Yo, thanks for cheering us up, Tom!! — Mr. Jolly Optimism, Mr. I-Know-Everything-About-Joe's-Life. Sheesh!!

Lookit, this guff may fool some Gloomy Gus lovers of great poetry, but not me, kiddo.

I went home to the theatre, and things are working out just fine, thanks!!

It's that reinvention thing again, I guess.

Feeling like I'd reached the, uh, acme of achievements in animation, and despite winning an award and getting a steady stream of unanswered cartoon-fan mail, I yearned to tread the boards once more.

At the prompting of many friends, I decided to do a one-man show. I asked Martin Olson to help me work up two or three viable vehicles and pitched them to a likely home for Ham, the Steve Allen Theatre. I was its hoping hip, young artistic director would pick the first one, which utilizes a cluster of original characters in a format so good, I don't even want to tell you the title!! Doesn't that sound cool?

But he was more interested in the other two, which involved me doing impressions, basically.

"Go with your strengths," everybody sang in unison.

"But I'm so tired of impressions," I wheedled wearily.

But then again, I knew they were right. That first idea was chancier in that it might draw a smaller audience than my return to proven territory, on which are camped a modest but loyal fan base. (But I'm determined to do that original-character show someday.)

So I opted for a show starring three of my least clumsy impersonations: Orson Welles, Vincent Price, and Lord Buckley. "Why not?" I figured. They're all favorites of mine, though in much different ways. Even more so, I liked the balance between their personalities.

I thought this three-character show had dynamic potential to spare, but recognized that it had no real unifying thread. So I set about finding one.

I saw that they all co-existed at the height of their powers only during the '50s, owing to the brief period of time that was Lord Buckley's reign. The most interesting year for Welles and Price in this decade was 1958, during which both had career turning points.

Welles had just made his last Hollywood masterpiece, *Touch of Evil*. And *The Fly*, co-starring Price, was a sci-fi sleeper which heralded his arrival as King of Horror Films.

For Richard Merle Buckley, 1958 was near the end of his life (but not his career).

"But who is this Lord Buckley guy anyway?" you may be wondering. Hopefully, this will be the last book in which this man needs any kind of introduction. He should not be a stranger to American culture. He was an outrageously original artist, a charismatic presence onstage and off, a visionary. Mixing his knowledge and love of literature and life with the hip poetry of jazz, he was a master of the spoken word whose recordings have influenced the very influential. Needless to say, His Lordship was a rare and tasty Ham!! Also, the legendary flows and ebbs of his colorful, inspirational personal life equals the biography of any performer from any era. (You have a computer? A bookstore gift certificate? Go do your homework.)

I first heard that voice in the mid-'60s. I bought his last album, used, for fifty cents, and wore it out on my record player over the next twenty years, spreading the word. Little did I know that he already had many other fans — no, *followers* — doing exactly the same thing.

Even more than Welles and Price, I knew the time had come for me to finally do Lord Buckley in public. I'd been rehearsing him for years, of course. So I decided to present a slice-of-life scene from each of their lives from that year and call it *1958: a Retrospeculation*.

I dug up a never-used piece of mine called "F for Funds" and refined it with Martin's help. In this sketch, Orson Welles, ensconced in his favorite Parisian bistro, is warned not to make any more long distance calls from his table. So, in order to raise money for his theatre work, he devises a way to call Luxembourg free. Then, while trying to arrange a date with a wealthy widow, he not only finds she's remarried, but the new husband's asking who's calling. Yet they charm each other into it anyway, Orson gets his way, and never even has to leave his table.

Vincent Price was known to haunt the college circuit, so I speculated a flaky film-school lecture for him in which he describes (in greater detail than usual) the true story of the worst — but funniest — day's shooting of his career. While filming the climax of *The Fly*, he couldn't keep a straight face when he heard the title monster's squeaky cries of "Help me!!" played on the set — and, by just retelling the story, he loses it all over again.

Now, every day of Buckley's life could be an adventure, and often was. So I chose to merely take a peek at one "typical" evening at home where, surrounded by friends, he entertains the gathering with one of his best flip history lessons, a spiritual romp called "The Gasser," the wigged-out story of a lost Spanish explorer who learns the secret of "the healing of the hands."

So now I had a show, but as I grew comfortable with the play's concept, I saw that I still had a handful of challenges to meet, although one task I could not complete.

Producing *1958* myself, I failed to lay the proper groundwork for publicity. I had to leave town for awhile due my sister's passing during the show's planning stages. But I decided to go ahead anyway, now more experimentally, as a warm-up to a more elaborate production down the line.

And despite the play's foreseeably small turnout, I'd like to think I came through on all the play's more creative challenges.

Co-directing and polishing material with Martin, many additions and revisions occurred naturally enough with the droll Welles and priceless Price portions of our program.

The Buckley segment was a challenge in itself, however, chiefly because there's so little of the man's performances on film or kinescope. To put it plainly, anyone playing Lord Buckley must pretty much *guess* how the man looked while doing his act!! As guidelines, I had the famous vinyl discs and access to the few clips of him doing his thing, but I had to personify a living, breathing Lord Buckley performing one of his historic routines on a typical night at home. Going by the tones and distance of his voice from his mic, by audience reactions and other subtle factors, I soon managed to reconstruct his physical being to everyone's (including my) satisfaction.

(I'm using abbreviations again: LB, OW & VP, okay?)

It was a good idea to contact his website, as it turned out. Michael Monteleone and Roger Mexico, who maintain lordbuckley.com, were extremely enthusiastic and supportive. Coincidentally, 2006 was LB's centennial birthday. So, these fellows were busy touring the country, visiting the many celebrations of LB's life and oeuvre. They also told me they were still searching for people who did him for a documentary they were (and are still) making. They call it *Too Hip for the Room.*

This wasn't just simple good timing on my part. Please consider that when I spoke to Michael and Roger over the phone to invite them to my show, their project had already been eleven years in the making!! Details about this docu's contents are best left to the film itself, but let me drop a few incredible names of those interviewed: Steve Allen, Jonathan Winters, Ken Kesey, Anita Page, Robin Williams, and many more, some now gone, whose lives were touched by LB and his family, either directly or indirectly.

I told them about *1958* and they vowed to not only come, but if it was deemed good enough, they'd send a film crew to record the show!! — which they eventually did.

The filmmakers also put me in contact with members of LB's family!! LB's truly cool grandson Trevor Cole, the musical effects designer for Nine Inch Nails, was the first to check me out. And in the third and closing segment, he saw and loved how I did "The Gasser." As LB himself might have said, this cat's grand-cat dug the scene, man!! And he in turn brought Lady Laurie, his Mom and LB's wise and devoted daughter. Described to me as "hard to please," she also thought my rendition of her flesh-and-blood Dad was one of the best she'd ever seen.

It's impossible to say how deeply this new bond with the man's own kin has affected me since. Words like "gratitude," not to mention "insight," barely express my feelings. We're all in accord that our joint goal is to spread the word of LB's vivid inspiration, which was the love that changed his life. (See the movie!!)

Suffice it to say that *1958* pleased those who saw it, especially the LB contingent. And my rewards were many: Not only did I make wonderful connections, but wonderful new friends; and not only did Michael and Roger film my show, they thought enough of my work to interview me for their film as well!! Therein, I discuss how I approach playing LB and his importance to the culture that is only beginning to acknowledge him. My lovely niece and personal assistant Trish learned a lot about theatre, helping me immensely during the economical (understaffed) six-week run.

I'm very proud to tell you I think I made a difference with this documentary. After years of trying to get Larry Storch, LB's most significant protégé, to participate, I suggested they drop my name and give it one more go. This time, he accepted their invitation. If I helped at all, fine; the important thing was to get Larry in this film, and they did get that done, thank God.

I've spoken with Larry myself a few times lately. Though age is catching up, he came alive for Michael and Roger's camera, as if reliving every moment. Knowing how seriously Mr. Storch takes Comedy, I'm not too surprised that the old spark still glows. And naturally, he hopes Lord Buckley will finally get the recognition he deserves.

Already slated for the Cannes Film Festival, we all hope *Too Hip for the Room* is finished and released soon. It should be an artistic and even civilizing landmark.

As I come to the end of my work up to now, WB has only just released a direct-to-DVD presentation: "Bah, Humduck! A Looney Tunes Christmas Original Movie." Ray DeLaurentis wrote and Charles Visser and Andrea Romano directed these unrated forty-six minutes, and although it's not bad, especially for kids, I had a sense of déjà vu about it. I guess that's due to the familiarity and popularity of the *original* original, Charles Dickens's "A Christmas Carol".

In this holiday frolic, I do Daffy as a mall magnate, Sylvester, Marvin, Pepe, and Foggy. Many more LTs (abetted by the current Talent Pool) are also on tap, making sure stubbornly stingy ol' Daf' learns lots of excruciatingly painful and embarrassing lessons along the way, including his first scene coming out of a toilet.

It's been airing on TV as well, I notice. So it should be a holiday classic in no time.

Additionally, Six Flags theme parks, lots more games like "Duck Amuck" (the latest one to date, based on the classic short) and web projects help keep the Looney Tunes' fame — and my income — alive.

As for now, where I find myself, I'm not returning to the toon mic exclusively. My recent reacquaintance with theatre has made me homesick for stand-up too.

So I'm working up a new act of old impressions, an hour's worth at least, and I hope to make a definitive recording of this material as well, doing what I can to reestablish poor, neglected Nostalgia and myself.

Well, that's a wrap. I couldn't possibly list, or even remember, all the rest of the work I've done.

Please forgive me if I've omitted anything important to you, my friends, co-workers and audiences alike. As a completist, if not a perfectionist, I tried my best to give readers my most meaningful, positive, and funniest memories, but —

Memory often fades with age, ya know? You forget where you've been, what you've said . . .

Chapter 21: Dedication

Does it matter where I express my ultimate gratitude? I prefer doing it here for some reason.

For career guidance, support and hard work, I must reiterate thanks to close friends and collaborators like Gary Rafferty, Martin Olson, and cousin Mark; to Ron Vawter for inviting me to explore theatre; to the Boston comedy scene, and radio royalty Loren and Wally.

In animation: Friz, Chuck, and June, and especially Bill Scott for taking me under his benevolent antler.

There are two basic definitions of dedication. The second is what you write in a book. Thanks, everyone, for helping me learn the first one.

As for my personal life, let me just say that the love and support of my immediate family has, in retrospect, proven to be worth even more to me than this crazy career of mine that they faithfully encouraged.

I'm as proud of my Mom Dorothy as much as she is of me. And my brother Ned, his agelessly beautiful wife Donna, and their sweet, smart, sensible daughters Christine, Tricia and Jackie, complete the circle of love we all enjoy. I am blessed. Did I mention the girls are all tall, gorgeous and unique? Remind me later, okay?

Dorothy, née Domenica Camille, my mother, from whom I inherited my larger-than-life performing talents and the drive to use them, can't wait to read this.

My brother Ned is a little worried about it, though. He thinks I'm gonna tell about the time he — Just kidding, babe. You've got such a great family, you have nothing to worry about.

Sadly, my sister, Dad and Mom are gone now, all within the past three years. Sad? We were devastated.

JoAnne Marie was a champion of charities, for the church and school for which she worked, then in many more communities, and then as a spokesperson for ovarian cancer survivors and related charities. She lived for many years with chemo, and became very influential, a comfort to those similarly stricken, and their families. I think she loved angels because I suspect she was one herself. I'll never forget her laugh; she was my best audience ever. And we never even had an argument.

My Dad, Joe Junior, shook hands with Jack Dempsey, hit three holes-in-one after retiring from the railroad and became a Kentucky Colonel. But much more importantly, he was one of those World War II heroes whose courageous exploits, with the famous 1276th Combat Engineers who liberated Europe, were only revealed near the end of his life. This was because his regiment, like the Marines, gave their word to each other to downplay all heroics back home, and even to refuse commendations along the way, though they were certainly qualified: Two-thirds of his original platoon were killed, and he himself saved at least three lives.

Domenica (Dorothy) Camille, my Mom, was smart, strong-willed, beautiful, caring and unquestionably the source of my talents, temperament and personality. Proud as I was of her, she wouldn't want me to say much more. Suffice it to say she will be greatly missed.

Before and after these tragic family passings, it was difficult for me to write this book, especially having been conceived as a humorous autobio, but as the brother and son of these good folks, I must thank them all, eternally, for all that they'd given — and still give — to me.

Well, for now, that's about it, I guess.

But just maybe . . .

This is no conclusion yet, people!!

Or if you prefer, —

That's *still* not all, folks!!

Appendix 1:
Joe Alaskey's Looney Tunes Checklist!!

I, Joe Alaskey, do solemnly swear that I have played all of the classic LT characters listed below at one time or another (including for toys, CD and video games, direct-to-DVD fare, live shows, feature films, and television).

All voices were originated by Mel Blanc (MB) unless otherwise noted (from my best research efforts).

BUGS BUNNY (incl. orig. version)
DAFFY DUCK (both darnfool-duck & greedy loser versions)
PORKY PIG (orig. v/o: Joe Dougherty)
ELMER FUDD (v/o: Arthur Q. Bryan)
SYLVESTER
TWEETY
FOGHORN LEGHORN (incl. all versions)
YOSEMITE SAM
MARVIN THE MARTIAN (incl. orig. ver.)
PEPE LePEW
SPEEDY GONZALES
ROAD RUNNER (usually a sound effect)
WILE E. COYOTE (Super-Genius)

HENERY CHICKENHAWK
BEAKY BUZZARD (orig. v/o: Kent Rogers)
CECIL TURTLE
CLAUDE CAT
CHARLIE DOG
BARNYARD DOG
TASMANIAN DEVIL
SYLVESTER, JR.
RALPH WOLF
SAM SHEEPDOG
K-9
GOSSAMER
FRISKY PUPPY
DODSWORTH (v/o: Benny Rubin doing Sheldon Leonard)
MAMA BEAR (v/o: Bea Benadaret)
CRUSHER (v/o: ?)
BABBIT & CATSTELLO (v/os: Tedd Pierce & MB)
HUBIE & BERTIE (v/os: MB & Stan Freberg)
MAC & TOSH (GOOFY GOPHERS / v/os: MB & Stan Freberg)
ROCKY & MUGGSY
COOL CAT (v/o: Larry Storch)
COLONEL RIMFIRE (v/o: Larry Storch)
MERLIN the Magic Mouse (v/o: Larry Storch)

I also rejuvenated plenty of memorable one-shot characters:

MICHIGAN J. FROG (*One Froggy Evening* / v/o: Bill Roberts)
PETE PUMA (v/o: Stan Freberg)
THE DODO (*Porky in Wackyland* / *Dough for the Do-do*)
TOM TURK (*Tom Turk and* Daffy / v/o: Billy Bletcher)

CASBAH (Bugs' romantic rival in *Hare Splitter*)
THE CONSTRUCTION WORKER (v/o: ?)
THE SHAKESPEAREAN DOG
THE STORK (Hic!!)
THE WEASEL (Slurp!!)
THE BIG GHOST (etc., laughing bully; v/o: Tex Avery)
THE GAMBLING BUG (v/o: Stan Freberg)
SAM (the *Birds Anonymous* sponsor cat)
HASSAN & THE SPIRIT OF THE LAMP (*Ali Baba Bunny*)
SLOPPY MOE (*Injun Trouble / Wagon Heels*)
McCRORY (*My Bunny Lies Over the Sea*)
J. EVIL SCIENTIST (*Water, Water Every* Hare / v/o: John T. Smith)
BRUNO (the Russian circus bear in *Big Top Bunny*)
BABY FACED FINSTER (*Baby Buggy Bunny*)
COUNT BLOODCOUNT (*Transylvania 6-5000* / v/o: Ben Frommer)
"MR. HYDE" versions of Bugs, Sylvester & Tweety
CALVIN Q. CALCULUS (*The Hole Idea*)
SLOWPOKE RODRIGUEZ (*Mexicali Shmoes*)
RALPH CRUMDEN (of The HoneyMousers / v/o: Daws Butler)

I've even used the voice of MEL BLANC himself now and then, most notably as Plucky's Dad on "Tiny Toons".

Of course, you can't do everything. Certain classic characters, many of them one-shots, were revivified by other Talent Poolers. The Ones That Got Away (so far):

MARC ANTONY (the bulldog from *Feed the Kitty*, etc.)
INJUN JOE (*Injun Trouble / Wagon Heels*)
SMOKEY the Genie (*A-Lad-in His Lamp* / v/o: Jim Backus)
PAPA BEAR (HENRY; v/o: MB & Billy Bletcher)

JUNYER BEAR (v/o: Stan Freberg)
THE GREMLIN (*Falling Hare*)
THE SHROPSHIRE SLASHER (*Deduce, You Say*)
DR. I. Q. HIGH (*Duck Dogers in the 24 ½th Century*)

Even More I'll Never Do (or ever be able to):

RALPH PHILLIPS (v/o: Dick Beals)
SNIFFLES (v/o: Bernice Hansen)
MISS PRISSY (etc. / v/os: various)
GRANNY (v/o: Bea Benadaret; June Foray)
WITCH HAZEL (v/o: June Foray)
MILLIE THE SLOBOVIAN RABBIT (v/o: June Foray)

Then are the ones who never had a voice!! So wish me luck!!

THE BOOKWORM
INKI
THE MINAH BIRD
PLAYBOY PENGUIN
EGGHEAD, JUNIOR
HIPPETY HOPPER

Appendix 2: Joe Alaskey's Favorites!!

Joe Alaskey's Top Ten Favorite Voice Actors
(in alphabetical order)

MEL BLANC
BILLY BLETCHER
PINTO COLVIG
HANS CONRIED
JUNE FORAY
PAUL FREES
STERLING HOLLOWAY
JACK MERCER
BILL SCOTT
BILL THOMPSON

Honorable Mentions: Jim Backus, Jackson Beck, Bea Benadaret, Robert Bruce, Daws Butler, John Byner, Kenny Delmar, Don Messick, Mae Questel, Gus Wickie

✳✳✳

Joe Alaskey's Top Twenty-Five Favorite Cartoons
(in chronological order)
[title / studio / year / director / star]

SNOW WHITE [Max Fleischer / 1933 / Dave Fleischer / Betty Boop, Koko, Bimbo]

A DREAM WALKING [Max Fleischer / 1934 / Dave Fleischer / Popeye, Olive Oyl, Bluto]

BROTHERLY LOVE [Max Fleischer / 1936 / Dave Fleischer / Popeye. Olive Oyl]

POPEYE THE SAILOR MEETS SINDBAD THE SAILOR [Max Fleischer / 1936 / Dave Fleischer / Popeye, Olive Oyl, Bluto, Wimpy]

GOONLAND [Max Fleischer / 1938 / Dave Fleischer / Popeye, Poopdeck Pappy, the Goons]

DER FUEHRER'S FACE [Walt Disney / 1943 / Jack Kinney / Donald Duck]

THE SWOONER CROONER [WB / 1944 / Frank Tashlin / Porky Pig]

SCAREDY CAT [WB / 1948 / Charles M. Jones / Porky Pig, Sylvester]

THE SCARLET PUMPERNICKEL [WB / 1950 / Charles M. Jones / Daffy Duck, all-star cast]

GERALD McBOING BOING [UPA / 1951 ? Robert Cannon / Gerald McBoing Boing]

RABBIT FIRE [WB / 1951 / Charls M. Jones / Bugs Bunny, Daffy Duck, Elmer Fudd]

CHOW HOUND [WB / 1951 / Charles M. Jones]

A BEAR FOR PUNISHMENT [WB / 1951 / Charles M. Jones / Three Bears]

RABBIT SEASONING [WB / 1952 / Charles M. Jones / Bugs Bunny, Daffy Duck, Elmer Fudd]

DUCK AMUCK [WB / 1953 / Charles M. Jones / Daffy Duck]

DUCK DODGERS IN THE 24 1/2th CENTURY [WB / 1953 / Charles M. Jones / Daffy Duck, Porky Pig, Marvin the Martian]

DUCK! RABBIT, DUCK! [WB / 1953 / Charles M. Jones / Bugs Bunny, Daffy Duck, Elmer Fudd]

RUGGED BEAR [Walt Disney / 1953 / Jack Hannah / Donald Duck, Humphrey]

CRAZY MIXED-UP PUP [Walter Lantz / 1955 / Tex Avery]

THE LEGEND OF ROCKABYE POINT [Walter Lantz / 1955 / Tex Avery / Chilly Willy]

SH-H-H-H-H [Walter Lantz / 1955 / Tex Avery]

ONE FROGGY EVENING [WB / 1955 / Charles M. Jones / Michigan J. Frog]

WHAT'S OPERA, DOC? [WB / 1957 / Charles M. Jones ? Bugs Bunny, Elmer Fudd]

BIRDS ANONYMOUS [WB / 1957 / I. Freleng / Sylvester, Tweety]

SHOW BIZ BUGS [WB / 1957 / I. Freleng / Bugs Bunny, Daffy Duck]

Honorable Mentions: Too many to mention!!

Appendix 3: Tips on Doing Impressions

Well, I committed myself to this, so there's no turning back now, I guess.

Look, it's simple: Most everybody has the potential, if not the desire, to do at least one good impression. Theoretically, I mean. I don't insist you try.

But let's say you've never tried doing one for anybody before. And now you want to, for reasons best known to yourself. Okay, here's how to go about it.

GO WITH YOUR STRENGTHS

Almost everybody resembles somebody famous, don't they? You've probably been told this once or twice, no? Or maybe you've been told you sound like so-and-so.

Well, if it's an actor (and it usually is), think of something you liked him or her in, and practice lines from his or her best work. The better known the movie or TV show, the better the audience's recognition factor.

The idea is: Use whatever advantage you have vocally and physically to sell your piece.

GO ALL OUT
Yes, to start with, be as hammy as you can be. Make faces and stretch your vocal chords to ridiculous extremes. And do it in a mirror first, for corn's sake, when nobody else is around.

Then pull your performance back till you find your greatest comfort level with the material. This will also determine the audience's greatest comfort level with you.

They might also like subtle stuff, but that depends on who you are, who you're doing, and how you're doing it.

KEEP THE WRITING SHORT AND SIMPLE
I used the Bad Casting routine. My particular spin on this standard bit is to find the worst possible roles, but ones that also somehow seem right, like a 180° spin that keeps you on track, just in reverse. For example: in the right costume, Don Rickles would *look a lot like* Charlie Brown!! You may not have realized it, but you *knew* it!! The premise imprints a simple but strong subliminal impression.

And I kept Bad Casting bits to about a minute each.

So find an original premise, if possible. Or spin an old one. Find a hook. Hone whatever puts the premise across best. And don't milk it too much — just enough.

SURPRISE THEM
— one way or the other, either in your choice of subject, style of humor, level of exaggeration, etc.

Don't be predictable. Assume audiences are smart; they prefer that. And with impressions, they can get 2 steps ahead of you in no time if you're not sharp and original.

If you can sing, or juggle, or whatever, use that too.

DON'T FORCE IT

If you've never tried doing an impression before, maybe it's because you're uncomfortable with the whole idea. If so, trust your instincts and go sit out front. We need audiences, baby.

But if you think you can be funny doing this, remember that *the audience wants to like you,* just like any other kind of performer. So be yourself, or a reasonable facsimile thereof, while establishing a rapport with people, which helps them feel more like an audience. If you're naturally shy, try writing about it, perhaps. If glitz and one-liners are your strengths, then do that.

But don't think you're smarter than the audience in any case. And if you lose them now and then, don't blame them. They can sense even latent hostility, so joking about their failure to respond can you get heckled.

Improvisation is fine if you can control it. But with impressions, you'll probably want a beginning, middle and end for each routine. Bottom line: Improvise while *writing.*

And while doing all that, think as originally as you can. If you like to play with a traditional format like I do with Bad Casting, be sure the folks can follow you, and will like the direction you're taking them in.

BE KIND

This is a style thing, and I have some nerve telling you it's better to work clean, but it's generally true.

You can be as snarky and satirical and scatological as you like. But again, remember: the audience does have a limit of acceptability as to what they'll tolerate. If you trash Johnny Cash in Nashville, you're hash.

And besides, your shock-wave excesses might come off looking worse than the people you're dissing. Then they might not like you as much!! (Also: Some celebrities sue!!)

Well, there ya go. Hope you can use these timple sips. "Get a good state job with a pension" is my real advice.

Appendix 4: A Joe Alaskey Short Story

Like my cartoons, my writings have been unpublished up to now. I'm very grateful to Ben Ohmart for not only taking on this book, but for offering me the space to print here, for the first time, one of my copyrighted short stories.

Thanks again should go to Richard Matheson, my primary inspiration, and still my favorite living, working writer.

As for the following story, I chose it because it's set in a world I understand, and because it's appropriate to this book. Hope you like it. And if you do, by all means, please enjoy it.

"Professional Courtesy"

A triple bypass. That's what he had to have. He wondered who was paying for it. Probably the daughter, by way of the son-in-law. Poor old Nat.

Zip folded up the trade paper and put it down on the coffee table. He thought about, for the nine-hundredth time, their personal history together. The old bastard. He hated to think of him suffering, dying slowly like this. They were about the same age. Zip didn't want to go that way, breaking up into little pieces, rotting in a hospital bed. No, that wouldn't be the way he'd go.

He remembered the good times. What few memories remained. Before the Big Time. The early stages, the clubs.

"What did Nat remember?" he wondered. He knew there were the beginnings of Alzheimer's. He'd read about that too, two years ago.

Zip couldn't help but reflect on the bad times, though. The arguments, the shoving match, the breakup. All so long ago. But just like yesterday, now they came back. He remembered the drinking, the women, the press junkets they had to do together. Comedy team — Feh.

And now Nat was almost gone. Might as well be dead, wasting away like that. A shame, no matter how they used to feel about each other.

Then he smiled. Because he knew Nat would always remember that Zip was the funny one. Nat was a good — no, a very good straight man. But funny? By himself? Get real. Zip got the laughs. Well, that's the patsy's job.

And they always knew it, both of them. They always knew each other's value, to the audience, to the studio, to each other. That was never in question. Comedy they knew. And Zip was always the funny one.

He proved that after the split. Then he had a career, a bigger and better career, and Nat retired. Oh, a few guest shots, a handful of walk-ons. That TV whodunit where he was the one whodunit. That was amusing, and Nat was a good enough actor to carry it off.

But then came the grey hair and those deep wrinkles. Laugh-lines, yeah. He'd aged badly.

Now, this surgery. Too bad.

Zip thought some more about that. He felt sorry now for the old bastard. Sure, he had to go, but Nat was just looking out for himself and his family. Was that so wrong? Was he worth more money back in '65? Yeah, probably. But business was business. Anyway, it was Morrie's decision, not Zip's. But it was a good decision, sound thinking.

But what a mess —

Oh, why hash over all that all over again? Didn't do Zip any good. Thank God *he* was still on his feet, still healthy. But he took care of himself after a point, and saved his money, invested it wisely. And Nat didn't. So now he was paying for it.

It really was too bad, though. Probably just a matter of time before he kissed off. The slow, painful, unhappy way... Really too bad.

So Zip had the money. Money Zip knew. Not Nat, though. Poor idiot, letting himself go like that with nothing to fall back on. Except the kids. Rotten shame.

Zip stood up and looked out at the pool. He put his hands on his hips and stretched his back.

He felt like doing something about it. They still talked once or twice a year. Maybe he should help. Maybe he'd call. He could get the number at the hospital, no problem. Of course, Nat wouldn't change that attitude, that bitter tone in his voice . . .

He looked at the grey TV screen, then down at the VCR.

Wait. Better yet . . .

"Let me sit up here," gurgled Nat.

The nurse, strong and pretty, if a bit fat, helped him sit up straighter against the pillows. One breast pressed against his face for a second, but Nat didn't really care. His lumbar was killing him.

How long had it been since the operation?

Eh. What did it matter? He didn't want to touch, didn't want to think about the thick stitches in his chest. All that dried blood and changing the dressing. Yecch. He never even looked. What a life.

"Need anything else?" the nurse asked.

"Naw, go on," he commanded. "Go freeze the bedpans."

She smiled crookedly. "Remember — Use the button. No yelling," she commanded back, and left.

Nat glanced over at his roommate. Out of commission. Poor shmo. Dying, like him, only closer to it now, since Friday. What was his name again . . . ?

Anyway, — a stroke. A coma. That's what Nat needed. Or another seizure, a nice, quick one. Biddy-*boom*. Get it over with.

Diane would be visiting later, about noon, he knew. Her and what's-his-name. Varkes. The Armenian. Couldn't marry a nice Jewish kid. No, she had to go Bohemian. Oh well, he was good to her. *And* him, he couldn't deny it. When he needed them, they were there. Thank God. Otherwise, where would he be? He sure couldn't count on his old friends. That bunch. No.

He wriggled a bit to make his lower half more comfortable. Stupid pajamas. Lousy, cheap, *farkakte* hospital. Well, it was better than nothing. Better than charity.

"Oy, what a life . . . I've lived too long," he said to himself for the nine-hundredth time.

He looked over at his tray. She forgot to take the tray, the stupid cow. No, she didn't forget. She wanted him to eat more. Huh. Forget it.

Then he saw the face. Right there in the mashed potatoes — The Star's face. The Big Star. Zip Schmip. Sherman, that bastard. The Movie Star.

How does that thing go, that song? "The Movie Star — and the rest . . ." That was him — the rest. Leftovers.

Nat sighed. Carefully. Disconsolately. Maybe he should kick up a fuss. Fall out of bed. Get this over with. Who could blame him? Who would care? He wished he could read his own obit in *Variety*. He wondered what they'd say — how much space he'd get. A paragraph. Three sentences maybe. Not even a picture. "Nat Barrows, Loser, Dies in Poverty at 85."

Not *him*, though. Not Zip Sherman, the Great Star. He'd get headlines in the trades, TV specials, a goddamn parade honoring his memory.

What a schmuck he'd been.

Oh, God, that itch again. He wouldn't scratch it. He wouldn't do even that much. To hell with it. He wasn't worth scratching, wasn't worth the effort . . .

He wondered if he'd call. He always got worked up when he heard that voice. Not that he'd ever give him the satisfaction of knowing that. But he couldn't help hoping the sonofabitch would call like he always did. Like they were still friends, like everything was still like the old days. No, he wouldn't let Zip have those years back. Wouldn't give him that satisfaction.

Still, Nat missed the laughs. The miserable bastard could always crack him up. That much he'd have to give him. Even if it was the laughter of bitter defeat. Zip always went for it, and Nat always cracked up. Not that anybody but them ever knew how hard it used to be for him to keep a straight face. Sometimes he lost it. Rarely onstage . . .

But in real life . . .

"Go away," he said to the itch. Then he scratched it with a harsh sigh.

At the Post Office, Zip stood looking at the slot for a moment, then pushed the package in. He rubbed his hands together; they felt wet. He swallowed and exhaled hard through his famous bell-shaped nose, and walked back out to the Silver Ghost. Jeeze, it was hot.

Those two old dolls were looking at him funny. He knew that look. He tipped his hat. They beamed. He fumbled with the keys. They chuckled, one shyly.

It was so easy. Still so easy.

Starting up the motor, he wondered if he'd done the right thing. Well, he had to do something to help out his old partner. To cheer him up. He drove away into traffic.

Nurse Fatty came back into Nat's room, a package under her arm.

"We're going to move Mister Christopoulos," she informed him as she approached the zonked-out old man. She checked his pulse and took his temperature. She had to close his mouth for him to do it.

"Don't let me stop you," Nat mumbled. "At least he's still getting mail."

She looked at the heart patient. "No, this is for *you,*" she smiled sideways and brought the package over to him.

He knew who it was from. He recognized the light brown paper, but inspected the return address anyway. Yep. Him.

But what was this? A book? Too light for a book. He squeezed the thing and turned it over in his hands.

"You trying to guess? Just open it!" she grinned.

"It's from him."

"I know. I read the name."

"Snoop. You *did* go through my wallet, didn't you?"

"You're paranoid, Mister Barrows . . . Aren't you going to open it?"

"Maybe . . ."

"All right, I'll go." She moved to the foot of the bed and retrieved a pillow instead.

Nat stared at the piece of mail as he tore it open.

"Huh. This is a tape . . . And there's a note."

He ignored her and read it as she stuffed the pillow behind him and cranked him up a bit.

"You want to know what he says?"

"I can see perfectly well what he says."

"Not much of a note, is it?"

"I think it's very nice. 'Thought you'd need a laugh.' Very thoughtful."

"Thoughtful, my ass. It's probably just him. He's still rubbing it in."

"Did you look at the label?"

"What label?" he sneered.

"On the tape! The one you're not looking at. It says: 'Sherman and

Barrows – Hollywood Starcase – 1962.'

"I don't remember doing that show — Wait. Yes I do. That French girl was on the show, the chantoose. And Gary Horton was the host."

"You mean 'Barry Horton'?"

"Yeah. Barry . . . the song-and-dance man. He was in Vaudeville."

"Would you like me to set up the VCR?"

"The what?"

"The tape machine. I can set it up in here for you."

"I remember this show. It was live. We did good. We wowed 'em."

"I'll set it up for you. Hand it over."

"You're going to charge me for that? For plugging in a machine? Is that fair?"

"No charge, Mister Barrows," the nurse lied. His son-in-law had paid for it. They just didn't want to upset the old man. "Don't upset yourself."

"Upset? Who's upset? I'm asking is all."

"It's our pleasure." She stood there waiting. "Give me the tape if you want to see it."

Nat gave her the tape and the wrapping paper.

"Throw it away."

"What, the tape?!"

"The note, idiot. And the paper."

"Oh. All right."

She turned on the set and pushed the tape into the slot. The tape began.

"Wait for the TV to go on, for God's sake."

"It's coming on now. See?"

"Throw the paper away."

She slipped the note into the tape's empty sleeve and crumpled up the brown paper, dropping it in his wastebasket as she handed him the RCU.

"Here's the remote. You remember how to use it?"

"I saw that, you sneak. Who wants to keep his lousy note? Not me. Take it out of that box."

"Stop making a fuss, Mister Barrows. And enjoy the show. I've got to finish my rounds."

"You're round enough already," Nat said after she left.

'Katherine Lesko, R.N.'. That was the name. He'd read the nametag. Again. He'd have to remember that from now on. She was good to him. Too fat but nice.

The sound got his attention. On came that announcer with that big voice. And the music.

"Live! From the Elysium Theatre in Hol-ly-wood! It's . . . The Hollywood Starcase! With this week's host! Barry Horton!"

There he was with the soup-and-fish, top hat and cane.

"And his guests . . . ! Sally Chase!"

Was *she* on that show? Oh, yeah, now he remembered meeting her there.

"Sherman and Barrows . . . !"

There he is, the bastard.

"Helene Auclair . . . !"

Of course. How could he forget? She had that great figure and those black bangs. Sexy.

Then jugglers, or acrobats, whatever they were. And some Navy band. And chimps, for God's sake. He recalled the filthy mess they made out of the Green Room.

"We'll be back after these words from our sponsor!"

Nat was looking at the remote control. He pressed 'Fast Fwd.' A car commercial came on, the new '63 Whoozits zooming by. He aimed the unit at the TV. Then the car went even faster.

He watched Barry Horton do "Everything's Coming Up Roses". With those girls. Good opening.

Then skipped the jugglers all in silk, and the toothpaste commercial. He watched half of the chimp act when he saw one dressed like the Marx Brothers — Groucho. Now there was a comic. There was a Star.

Then some nonsense with the audience. Horton's old singalong bit. Then he zipped by the next car commercial.

Zip — There he was. They were on.

"Where's the whattyacallit?!" he fretted.

'REW.' Was that it? He pushed the button. The tape rewound so he could see it from the beginning. The act, the old act. It was the Soap Box routine. Must've been election time. He watched. He smiled . . .

Zip Sherman woke up and answered the phone. It was Gabe Landon from the Times. He turned on the lamp, sat on the sofa and listened. Then he gasped and moaned and eulogized briefly, something quotable he'd written that afternoon.

"Died laughing, did he? Well, at least he went happy."

Of course he'd be going to the services. No matter what they said about them, he'd always considered Nat his friend . . .

When he hung up, he knew he'd done the right thing.

Jos. Alaskey
© 2004

They say: 'He who laughs last laughs best.'

Then again, they also say: 'Laughter is the best medicine.'

Zip simply put the two together and decided that Nat's last laugh would be the best medicine of all.

(Thank you, OTR Announcer.)

In choosing which story to include as a sample of my work, I just

Appendix 5:
Joe Alaskey's Got a Swelled Head

— a pounding headache, actually, from all this typing and proofreading. Sheesh!!

But just for yocks, here are some interesting FACTOIDS about me that I couldn't quite work into the text.

- Daffy Duck and I actually share the same birthday!! "Porky's Duck Hunt", his first theatrical short, was released on April 17, 1938. And exactly fifteen years later, so was I.

- The little curlicue thing I scrawl under my signature was cribbed from John Hancock's more famous one, and in my case it means "III (the third)".

- I once threw a penny on its edge in full view of three witnesses. I was paying for morning coffee at a diner. One of my friends and both proprietors (a married couple from Korea) watched me toss some change on the counter-top. And one cent stood straight up. The owners steppedback and gasped, and later built a little wall of condiments around it to preserve it for good luck. The little shrine lasted a few weeks, during which time, "Twilight Zone" fans, I mysteriously acquired the ability to read Dick York's mind.

- I found a four-leaf clover once, too. Mom still has it.

- Modesty prevents me from mentioning the actual amount, but I once made a flabbergasting five-figures per word at a recording session for a live network TV spot!! One of the two words was "despicable". Can you guess the other?

- Who doesn't like board games? In my spare time, I've developed a few over the years, and to everyone's surprise, they work!! So don't be surprised if, some time in the future, you hear I've sold one (if you're that interested). You might see my latest pitch, based on a classic comic strip, on toy store shelves by Christmas. Who knows?

- Of historical interest: My Bugs Bunny voice was the first ever heard on an international phone-patch hook-up. The inventor had me speak to some Japanese businessmen. They spoke no English, but gleefully recognized the voice!!

- And here's a list of unusable words coined for this book:

Word	Page #
Abominably Snowbound, the	13
alliterrhea	86
aniboom, cel-shocked	64
animaven	55
Bardwise, facsimiloquist	31
clansbabe	80

comediturge	29
dialects-pert, polyvox	7
Digital Aged, the	63
Funnymanifest Destiny	51
hamwork	19
sagebrushed	110
thumbwise	108
toonwise	93
webward, webworks	88

If anyone else came up with any of these words first, and can prove it, my apologies. I only read cereal boxes.

And if you don't like Freedom of Speech, feel free to shut up!! (My wittiest bad joke . . . You're welcome.)

As for me using double exclamation points instead of the standard single unit, I only do this when it's me personally talking. And they aren't in my short stories because I opt to observe standard narrative rules.

Personally, though, I have no real reason, nor any real apology, for doing this, except that it's just an idiosyncrasy that began in my cartooning, to tell you the truth, and carried over into stuff like this.

I also center eleven asterisks at the end of whatever I write because eleven's my lucky number, and because I like asterisks a lot.

If any of this annoyed you, you can always go back through the book and blot out all the extra punctuation.

As for future works, watch for more inane time-wasters like: stage plays, puzzle books, cartoon books, short story anthologies, ad nauseum. Because I'm gonna keep righting till I get it write!!

Well, thanks for reading this far. You can stop now.

Go doodle on the blank page.

Bear Manor Media

$19.95 — Rocking Horse: A Personal Biography of Betty Hutton

$19.95 — Any Way I Can: 50 Years in Show Business By John Gay

$19.95 — acting foolish — lewis j. stadlen

$24.95 — Confessions of an Accidental Mouseketeer

$19.95 — Branson's Country

$14.95 — The Philip Rapp Joke File by Philip Rapp, Edited by Ben Ohmart

$19.95 — Angelic Heaven: A Fan's Guide to Charlie's Angels by Mike Pingel

$19.95 — Spotlights & Shadows: The Albert Salmi Story by Sandra Grabman

$19.95 — Talking to the Piano Player 2: Stars, Writers, and Bandleaders Remember by Sheal Coleman

$19.95 — Through a Lens Darkly by Jan Wahl

Check out our latest titles!

For details on these, and nearly a hundred other books, visit

www.bearmanormedia.com

Add $5.00 shipping for the first book, $1.00 for each additional book

Please join our online mailing list for news and coupons!
http://groups.google.com/group/bearmanor

BearManor Media • PO Box 71426 • Albany, GA 31708